Dr John Pearce

GOOD HABITS,
BAD HABITS

*Stopping bad daytime and night-time habits
and encouraging good ones*

Thorsons
An Imprint of HarperCollinsPublishers

To Mary

Thorsons
An Imprint of HarperCollins*Publishers*
77–85 Fulham Palace Road,
Hammersmith, London W6 8JB
1160 Battery Street,
San Francisco, California 94111-1213

Published by Thorsons 1994
1 3 5 7 9 10 8 6 4 2

A catalogue record for this book
is available from the British Library

ISBN 0 7225 2296 7

Printed in Great Britain by
HarperCollinsManufacturing Glasgow

Contents

· · · · ·

INTRODUCTION
· · · · ·

'If he does it once more I will scream.' Habits provoke strong reactions in people and even stronger emotions in parents who observe their child repeat the same movement or say the same thing over and over again. Children who have a habit that is obvious in public, such as sniffing or twitching, can be particularly embarrassing to their parents who feel guilty and wonder what they have done to deserve this.

In spite of the strong feelings that habits can cause, they are so frequent that every one of us has several habits, even though most of them are unconscious and we perform them without any thought.

Although it is easy to think of habits as being either bad or useless, most of the habits that we have as adults are good ones. Fortunately, it is possible to train children to have good habits and this book tells you how you can do this.

The word 'habit' means a learned behaviour that is repeated frequently and comes from the Latin word *habitus*, meaning a custom. The term covers a wide range of behaviours including rituals, routines, tics and obsessions. It seems likely that they share many characteristics in common and have an underlying physical component in the brain. That habits are related to the workings of the chemicals and nerves in the brain may sound a bit worrying, but many of our habits and routines help us to cope with life so that we don't have to think about every small detail that we repeat each day.

The close relationship between the brain and habits is one of the reasons why people mistakenly believe that when children bite their nails or twitch or repeat any habit again and again, it must be a sign of emotional disturbance. Fortunately this is rarely the case.

This book tells you how children's habits are formed and why some children are more likely to develop habits than others. You will find how to help your child to develop good habits and how to deal with the bad ones that can cause so much embarrassment and distress.

One of the first habits to be established in children is the routine that develops around bedtime and sleeping. A good sleep habit is so important for children and for a happy family life. Because bad sleep habits cause so many problems for parents, a whole chapter of this book is devoted to sleep, with clear guidelines on how to deal with childhood sleep problems.

However, this book is mainly about the ordinary habits of everyday life that are not a major worry, but which could become fixed habits that continue right into adult life. There are simple guidelines that you can follow so that you can help your child develop the good habits and lose the bad ones.

You might ask, 'Why do parents need to read a book on habits? They are only a passing phase anyway, surely it is best to take no notice of them and they will naturally fade away?' This approach certainly works for some children, but for others the habit may be in the form of a tic or an obsession that may not fade away on its own so easily.

Over the past few years there have been great advances in the understanding of how habits are formed and what to do about them. It is no longer necessary to just hope that your child will grow out of a bad habit. It can be really helpful for parents to know how best to manage a habit, rather than keeping their fingers crossed and hoping for the best.

Unfortunately, the complete information on habits, tics and

obsessions isn't easily available to the general public, mostly because research is published in so many different scientific journals. New understandings about habits and how best to deal with them is therefore difficult for parents to get hold of. In writing this book I have used the best of the research findings and I have also used all the guidelines myself in my work with children and families.

You may be surprised to find that most, if not all of the suggestions that I make sound like basic common sense. This should reassure you, but many busy parents find that so-called 'common sense' is not that easy to come by. In any case, experts don't always agree. At least you will know that the approaches outlined in this book are based on many years of practical experience, helping children to develop good habits and teaching parents how to deal with the bad ones.

I would like you to feel that I am talking directly to you as you read through the book. You can 'talk' back to me if you don't agree with what I have said or if you don't understand. Then read on and it should become clear why I have taken a certain line rather than any other. Don't hold back from having an argument with me in your head or asking someone else what he or she thinks. In this way you will become much clearer about what you believe yourself.

Childcare is not so much about right and wrong, but more about finding the best compromise between the various demands of family life. For this reason it is impossible to 'get it right' all the time and this often leads to feelings of guilt. In fact, a normal part of being a parent is feeling guilty about not always doing the right thing for your child!

If you are unsure about your own ideas, but have some reservations about what I have written, I would like you to follow my suggestions as closely as possible, in spite of any reservations you might have. I have been very careful to give guidelines and advice only where I am confident that it is safe, reasonable and effective. If you have followed the guidelines carefully and they have still not worked, please don't immediately think that I have got it all wrong. It is much more likely that you haven't been sticking closely enough to what I have said. So read the book again, have another go...and don't give up!

It is the love you have for your child that makes being a parent so fulfilling and joyful. But it is this same bond of affection that makes it so painful and distressing when things go wrong. Having a child with a nasty or embarrassing habit can make a parent's feelings of love change to frightening feelings of rejection all too easily. Fortunately it isn't necessary to love your child all the time in order to be a reasonable parent.

At the end of the book there is a section outlining some of the research on habits, tics and obsessions for those of you who would like to have more details and to read further on the subject. I hope that there is something of interest for everyone, even if you have no children. You might even find out something about your own habits, most of which can be traced back to childhood.

1

· · · · ·

Making Life Easier!

Habits form an important part of our everyday life: getting up in the morning, dressing, eating meals, going to bed at night and so on. We all have our own routines that are repeated day in and day out so that they become unconscious habits. This is just as well because it would be very difficult to have to think about every single action, like whether to brush your teeth before or after washing or whether to put the left sock on first or the right one. Here are some examples of daily habits that occur naturally and without much thought:

- lying in a particular way when going to sleep
- always holding a knife and fork in the same way
- starting to walk with either the left or the right foot first
- waking up at the same time each morning without an alarm clock
- sitting in a preferred position
- blowing the nose in a particular way.

These routines and habits make life that much easier because they become automatic – leaving space to think about more important things. At the same time the repetition and boring sameness of habits gives a feeling of security and predictability about life that can be very helpful, especially at times of stress. Children are not born with their habits already made. Habits and routines can only develop by being repeated over and over, again and again. And the sooner a child gets into the family routine for daily activities the easier it will be for all concerned.

The main habits and routines of daily living will be covered in this chapter, but going to bed and sleeping are dealt with in Chapter 3. Bedtime habits need to be sorted out early on, otherwise it may be difficult to establish a happy family life. The daily habits that I will deal with in this chapter are:

- eating and drinking
- being clean and dry
- dressing and undressing
- keeping clean and tidy (washing, brushing and nose-blowing)
- sitting still and paying attention
- keeping safe
- having good manners.

HOW TO MAKE GOOD HABITS

Whatever good habit you would like to encourage in your child, the ways to go about it are the same. The making of good habits requires a determination to keep going on and on training your child. But in the end, perhaps after many months or even years, your efforts will be rewarded and you will find that you no longer have to bother about the boring details of everyday life.

Repetition – Any behaviour that is repeated enough times will eventually become a habit and happen automatically. This is one reason why bad habits need to be stopped as early on as possible, before they have been repeated too many times.

A running commentary — When you are training your child in a new habit a running commentary can reinforce the behaviour. Sometimes it helps to tell your child what is going to happen before you get your child to carry out the habit.

Keeping to a routine — Habits are more likely to develop if the behaviour is always repeated in the same order and as part of the same daily routine at the same time of day.

Using counting and the clock — The timing of habits is also important. There is no point in working hard to establish a good habit only to find that your child takes ages to carry it out. Counting up to 10 or some other number, or using a clock or an alarm can be very effective in setting the time limit for any behaviour. Counting has the advantage that it can be slowed down or speeded up as you wish.

Taking it seriously — Children are quick to realize if their parents are not very serious about what they say and will take advantage of this by doing their own thing. Although it may seem silly to give the boring details of everyday routines much thought, children won't get into any good habit unless they believe that you know what you are doing.

But not too seriously! — If your children get the feeling that you have a big emotional investment in their habit, they will use it to wind you up if you are not very careful. Try and keep a sense of humour even when your children are testing you out.

EATING AND DRINKING

Drinking habits are the first to be learnt. If the milk tastes different or isn't at the usual temperature, the baby will probably complain. Babies will soon let you know if they are not being held in a familiar way or if there is anything else that is different from usual.

Small babies are often fed on demand, but if you allow this to continue for too many months, it will eventually become a habit and your child will demand food at all times of the day and night. By six months of age it is helpful to have made a start in training your child into the habit of having regular mealtimes.

The fact that your child comes to expect meals at certain regular times may seem as though you will become a slave to these times. It isn't as bad as it seems because once you have established a good mealtime habit, it is then possible to have occasions when you can change the routine without losing the good habit. The alternative of not having regular routines and habits for mealtimes is to have disorganized, stressful meals and a child who demands food and drinks at all times of the day and night.

You will need to have a very clear idea about what eating habits you would like your child to have. What type of foods and drinks, what table manners? It is important that all adults in the household agree on what standards are to be expected. It is a waste of energy trying to make a good habit for a child if the parents don't agree about it.

If you don't want your child to be a fussy eater, you will have to work hard at slowly introducing new foods as your child grows older. Almost all food likes and dislikes and other eating habits are developed during childhood. So it is best to sort them out early on, because the longer a habit continues, the more difficult it is to change (see my book *Food: Too Faddy, Too Fat* in this series).

14

Most children show clear preferences for certain foods from an early age and tend to avoid food that has a strong flavour. But it is possible to alter children's taste for foods by being selective. The foods that you give your child to eat will shape his or her likes and dislikes for taste, texture and temperature in the future.

The process of learning good eating habits takes many years, so don't feel in any rush or get into a panic about a child who is fussy with food. If you work on it steadily you should win through in the end.

BEING CLEAN AND DRY

Gaining control over the bowels and the bladder is a skill that develops over the first few years. Most children are reasonably clean by the age of three years and dry by day at four years and by night at five years. Boys tend to take a bit longer than girls to become clean and dry and there are many other reasons for a delay in bowel and bladder control (see my book *Growth and Development* in this series).

Although most children have the ability to have some control over their bowels by a year and their bladder by 18 months, it is reasonable to start to train a good toilet habit before that. There is some evidence that waiting for control to develop naturally leads to delay in becoming dry and clean.

When children are able to sit unsupported it is a good idea to have them sit on the potty regularly at nappy-changing time. In this way the first habit of toileting will get well established before the second stage, which is actually 'performing' on the pot.

If you start your child sitting on the potty from the early age of nine months or so, it will give you lots of time to get the sitting habit fixed without having to start later when children go through the phase of tempers and saying 'no' to everything.

Occasionally your child will, by luck more than any other

reason, actually do a pee or a poo in the pot – which then gives you the chance to jump up and down with excitement and give lots of praise. This starts the process of the training for a good toilet habit that will then need to be carried on for as long as it takes – which may be a year or more.

Children take much longer to be confidently clean and dry than is generally recognized and accidents can easily occur. If, after becoming clean and dry, a child has a relapse for whatever reason, it may be necessary to repeat the toilet training sessions again:

- STAGE 1: Sitting on the toilet regularly for three minutes as often as it requires to keep clean and dry.
- STAGE 2: Having plenty of praise for any success in the toilet.
- STAGE 3: Having plenty of praise for being clean and dry.
- STAGE 4: Helping to clear up any accidents (if the child is old enough).

If your child has got into a bad toilet habit and either refuses to sit on the potty or wets and soils after the age when most children are clean and dry – don't despair, there is a lot that can be done to help. You may be told: 'Don't worry, the child will grow out of it.' This could well be true, but it is not good enough if a child is still having daytime toilet problems when starting at school, or night-time problems with wetting at seven years old.

Toileting problems can cause great distress and need to be dealt with before they begin to interfere with a child's social and emotional life. There are many ways of helping children gain a good toilet habit. The principles are the same as for all habits and involve the four stages outlined above. Most important of all the principles is to *avoid distressed emotions about habits*. Try and keep your approach straightforward, down-to-earth and practical with a sense of humour. It may be difficult to do this when faced with soiled or wet clothes, but getting upset or cross about it will only make matters worse. (For further details about what can be done to help children who continue to wet or soil see *Growth and Development* and *Successful Potty Training* in this series.)

DRESSING AND UNDRESSING

One-year-old children are already beginning to help with dressing by lifting an arm or leg up. It isn't long before they become *too* helpful with undressing and remove clothes when they are not meant to. By the time children start at school it is best if they are able to cope with putting clothes on, taking them off and maybe even managing buttons. Laces are more difficult and it isn't until about seven to eight years of age that most children can do laces up.

Most children go through a phase of being difficult about dressing. This is when it helps to make sure that they already have a good dressing habit. This will mean always dressing in the same way and making it into a ritual. When children are still young (less than six to eight years old), it is best to avoid long discussions about what a child will wear today. Choice of clothing is best left until after a good dressing habit has been established. Here are some ideas on how to make dressing into a habit:

- Always dress your child with the same approach.
- Put clothes on and take them off in the same order.
- Give a running commentary as you go along – 'first you put the right arm in, then you put the left one in', 'over the head it goes and then tuck it in' and so on.
- You decide which clothes your child will wear – until the dressing habit is established.

- The habit can be reinforced by asking your child 'now what is next?'
- As your child develops a good dressing habit it is important to do less and less yourself, otherwise you will become part of your child's habit!

This may sound very artificial and boring and to some parents it may even seem too organized and repressive. But the alternative is to have long discussions and perhaps even arguments every morning about what clothes your child will wear. Which is fine if you enjoy arguing and have the time. Your early efforts to make a good dressing habit routine for your child will pay off later and it is well worth working hard to achieve.

KEEPING CLEAN AND TIDY

Learning clean habits is important for both health and social reasons. Dirty children do get teased and picked on at school, but to keep an active and boisterous child clean and tidy can be an exhausting job. The sooner being clean can be made into a habit routine, the better.

All the rules for making habits also apply to being clean. You need to make it absolutely clear exactly how you would like your child to wash, to clean his teeth, to blow her nose and so on. Even the way children are expected to wipe their bottoms has to be made clear and must be practised until it becomes an automatic habit.

Sometimes parents are surprised to find that they are not quite sure themselves which is the correct way to be clean. In fact there are many different ways, but if you feel at all unsure, then ask around your friends. You will be interested to find how many alternatives there are. In the end you will have to choose the methods that you feel are the best.

The first step in helping a child to develop a good habit routine for keeping clean is for the parent to do it for the child, repeating it over and over again in exactly the same way each time, with the same running commentary describing what you are doing. Then, as your child becomes old enough, you can gradually allow him or her to do more and more — at first under your supervision and then quite alone.

This is a process that normally takes years to achieve. Children don't have the co-ordination that is necessary for washing properly until five to seven years, and even then many children will still find it difficult to blow their noses, brush their teeth, or wash behind their ears and other vital parts!

Hair-brushing is another habit that requires a great deal of co-ordination and it isn't until 8 to 10 years old that children have the necessary skills to make a reasonable job of it — even when really trying hard.

Don't be fooled by your child being able to wash alone on a few occasions and think that supervision can now be stopped. Most children find that keeping clean is very boring and they will avoid it if possible. Even after 10 years of developing clean and tidy habits most children still need some supervision from time to time.

Spot-checks are a good way of doing this, so that children are never quite sure when they will be checked up on. Of course the checking has to stop eventually, but on the whole it is better to do it later rather than sooner. Finding the right time to fade out supervision is one of the great arts of being a parent.

SITTING STILL AND PAYING ATTENTION

Strange as it may sound, children need to be taught to sit still and pay attention. Most children don't do this naturally, but if regularly instructed in how to remain still, it will eventually become a habit. Young children under five years old are naturally active, which can put them at risk of harm. For this reason we have stair gates, walking reins and play pens. These offer control, but do not teach good habits.

Children need to learn the habit of sitting still before they go to school, because it is difficult to learn when on the move. Certainly reading requires children to stay still and pay attention.

Mealtimes are good for developing a sitting habit. Children will soon learn to sit still if that is the only time that they are given food and the food is removed if they get down from the table. Another good time to practise a good sitting-still habit is when you read to your child. Again your child will soon learn the habit if you only read when there is no wriggling about.

Young children can only sit still and pay attention for quite short times. A reasonable guideline is to expect children to be able to do this for the number of minutes that matches their age – with a maximum number of minutes that is double their age:

- 3 years: 3–6 minutes
- 5 years: 5–10 minutes
- 7 years: 7–14 minutes
- 10 years: 10–20 minutes.

Obviously, the time that a child can be still and pay attention will depend on many different factors, such as:

Gender. Generally, boys find being still more difficult than girls do.

Interest factor. It is easier to be still and concentrate if it is interesting or exciting for the child.

Distractions. It is difficult to pay attention if there are interruptions or diversions.

Ability to concentrate. Some children naturally concentrate better than others.

Emotional state. A distressed child will find it difficult to be still and pay attention under any circumstances.

Being still is the first step in learning the habit of concentration. If children are on the move, rushing around the place, there is little hope that they will concentrate for long. Most parents help their children to develop the habit of sitting still without having to do very much, but if your child is taking a long time to learn the habit, you can help your child in the following ways:

1. Start when your child is still young – even before learning to walk.
2. Try to be relaxed and still yourself.
3. Have short periods of holding your child quietly.
4. Start with a few seconds and gradually increase the time, using the guidelines above.
5. Aim for your child to be able to sit still at your side before four years old.
6. Finally, aim for your child to be still without being near you before starting at school.
7. Make these exercises good fun and keep to the times indicated above.

The habit of being still is really very important for children when they start school, so it is best to start early, repeating the exercise as often as necessary to get the habit well established. Some children are very restless when they are young and you may have to hold on to them quite firmly, otherwise they will wriggle away. But whatever you do, don't lose your sense of humour or get angry.

As soon as children have got into the habit of sitting still for short periods, you can move on to helping them to pay attention. One of the best ways of doing this is by playing simple games and gradually building up your child's attention span by using more and more complicated games and extending the time limit for the game without falling into the trap of allowing the game to go on for too long.

KEEPING SAFE

Helping your child to have good safety habits is obviously important and can mean the difference between life and death. Here are some common dangers for which children need to develop safety habits as early on as possible:

- electricity
- gas
- heat and fire
- water
- heights
- machines
- animals
- roads
- strangers.

Children have to develop their own safety habits for each of these dangers. This means that parents will have to go through the routine for teaching good safety habits again and again until they are sure that their child really is as safe as possible.

It is important to check constantly that your child's safety habits are still in good shape. Here are some ideas about how this can be done:

- Watch your child's behaviour when near danger, without making it obvious that you are watching.
- From time to time ask your child to repeat to you what the safety habit is.
- Carry out spot-checks to see what your child actually does when you are not around.
- If you are not completely satisfied, the safety habit will need to be practised a bit more.
- Use every opportunity to talk about and to repeat the safety habit.

- Remember that children take many years to develop a safety habit; even teenagers can't be fully trusted and will need some supervision.

HAVING GOOD MANNERS

It certainly helps children to get on well in life if they are polite and have good manners. However, what is regarded as good behaviour in some families would be thought of as very odd in others. It is more helpful to teach 'automatic' habits of good manners than to have long discussions about them, because children can't easily understand why one behaviour is better than another – it isn't always easy for adults to see any logic to some so-called 'good manners', either!

Here are some guidelines for teaching the habits of good manners and politeness:

- All the adults in the family must agree on what constitutes good manners.
- Be very clear about what standards of behaviour you expect.
- Set a good example yourself.
- Repeat the good manners over and over again.
- Keep at it until you find that your child is doing it automatically.
- Children often need to be reminded about good manners and you may need to do a short 'refresher course' for your child if necessary.
- There is no point in being angry if your child forgets to have good manners. All that the child needs is more practice.

CONCLUSION

Good habits have to be made, but once made life becomes easier and safer. It is very easy to see your child doing something once and think that a good habit is now fixed. However, most children seem to be better at remembering bad habits than remembering the good ones! Repetition and supervision may still be needed many years after a good habit has been learnt. So never give up!

2

. . . . .

How to Deal with Children's Common Bad Habits

No one should be surprised that children develop habits since we all have at least one or two ourselves. These habits often annoy other people but are quite comforting to perform and this makes them difficult to stop. Even something as simple as thumb-sucking can cause upset and annoyance for some people. The most common annoying or antisocial habits are shown below:

- thumb- and finger-sucking
- using a comforter
- head-banging
- rocking
- nail-biting and -picking
- nose-picking
- sniffing
- skin-picking and scratching
- lip-licking.

Each of these little habits can start off as a normal response to hunger, itching, boredom, irritation or some other good reason. Unfortunately, the behaviours only have to be repeated a few times to soon become fixed as a habit.

All habits tend to vary in how severe they are, but the list above serves as a reminder that even apparently harmless habits like nail-biting can be difficult to stop. Many children have had one or more of these habits for years in spite of repeated attempts by their parents to stop them. The problem is that habits develop easily and then become stuck. Here are some of the reasons why this happens:

- The original cause, such as an irritation, is still present.
- The habit gets attention for the child.
- Other family members have the same habit, so it is copied.
- The habit is familiar and comforting.
- The habit gives a feeling of security.
- People keep drawing attention to the habit.

Another problem with habits is that if you draw attention to them they generally become worse, but if you ignore them, this will have little or no effect either. However, there are three conditions that actually make habits worse:

1. distress and emotional upset
2. excitement and over-arousal
3. boredom and lack of stimulation.

Unfortunately most children spend a lot of time in one of these three states, so it may be difficult to find a time when your child is just 'normal' and in the best mood to stop the habit. We talk about 'breaking' a habit – this gives some indication of just how hard it can be to stop habits.

Looking on the bright side of things, most of these bad habits are passing phases of development and most children do grow out of them. Quite normal children can have any or all of the habits mentioned without being disturbed or insecure in any way. It is only where the habit is very severe or prolonged that parents should consider whether the time has come to do something to help the habit fade away.

WHEN TO DEAL WITH A HABIT

Habits are such a normal part of growing up that many parents don't worry about their child's little habits. Parents may actually encourage the habit by putting a comforter or thumb in the mouth to keep a child quiet, or by continually drawing attention to the habit: 'There you go – you're doing it again.' Any bad habit may be socially embarrassing at some time or another and many of them can cause damage to the body if they are repeated over and over again. I will discuss each of the most common habits separately, but here are some general points to be considered before deciding whether to do anything about a habit:

- Have most other children of the same age grown out of the habit?
- Is your child being teased about the habit?
- Is the habit causing any damage to the child?
- Does the habit make you so upset that you can't ignore it?

If the answer to any of these questions is yes, then read on because it is probably worth while trying to do something to stop the habit – or at least reduce its frequency.

THUMB AND FINGER HABITS

One of the first things that a new-born baby does is to put its fingers or thumb in its mouth and then suck. This natural reflex may remain as a lifelong 'mouthing' habit. For example, nail-biting and smoking are based on this early habit. Most, but not all, children go through a finger/thumb phase and there is little point in becoming upset about such a normal habit in the first two to three years of childhood.

So why bother at all about these sucking habits? Here are some reasons why (and when) the habits may interfere with normal life and even become a handicap for a child:

- They make the mouth or fingers sore – any age.
- They make communication difficult – any age.
- They put the mouth out of shape – after the age of 2–4 years.
- They make an older child look immature – after 5–7 years.
- They become a target for teasing – after 5 years old.

Although there is probably no truth in the belief that children will become disturbed if you prevent them from thumb-sucking, there is no point in making it into a major battleground because that will lead to other forms of problem behaviour. However, if your child seems to have become dependent on sucking in almost every situation, if it has caused some soreness around the mouth or if your child is about to start school it is worth trying at least to reduce the frequency of the behaviour.

Here are some ideas that you can try out, but please don't let it make you upset if they don't work – just try again later. The more that emotions become mixed up in habits the worse they become, so don't take them too seriously. I will refer to thumb-sucking only, but the same approach applies for finger-sucking just as well.

- Try and keep your child's hands occupied with other things so that they are not available for sucking.
- If you see the thumb in the mouth, give your child something to carry that needs the hands, without saying anything about the sucking.
- Say nothing, just casually reach out and remove the thumb from the mouth and carry on as if nothing has happened.

- It may help to put some kind of reminder on the thumb, such as a bit of sticky plaster, or you could draw a dot or a face on it.
- Another method involves training a child to identify the 'at risk' times for sucking and to hold the thumb at these times while counting up to 20.
- Provide something else for the child to hold when going to sleep, such as a teddy bear or a soft toy.
- If all else fails, but only if your child agrees and is motivated, it may help to strap the thumb to the side of the hand with sticky plaster, so that it can't be sucked during the night. Make sure that it doesn't restrict the blood flow by being too tight and take it off during the day.

Strapping the thumb or the fingers together may sound a little extreme, but thumb-sucking is impossible for children to control when they are asleep. Sometimes children are very keen to stop sucking but can't help themselves and do it automatically without thinking. In this case most children will welcome the strapping with sticky plaster as being helpful, especially if you can think of a way of making it into a joke.

Certainly if the hand or mouth is becoming sore or if your dentist says that the mouth is growing so that the jaws are out of line, some form of prevention of further sucking will be helpful. But the habit is never worth getting too worked up about or being cross with your child about.

COMFORTERS

Most children go through a phase, usually between one and two years old, when they like to put all sorts of things in their mouths. This is one way that children use to explore the world around them. However, because the mouthing is repeated over and over again it can easily become a habit.

Parents often encourage the habit of putting things in the mouth because they soon find that their children seem to be much more peaceful and quiet with something in the mouth. Sometimes children develop the most amazing habits that involve holding or twiddling a bit of themselves or something soft and cuddly while at the same time sucking a finger or thumb.

A comforter is an object that the children use to make themselves feel more settled and secure. It comes to represent the security that would normally be provided by a parent, so children use comforters more frequently if they are going to be away from their parents for any reason.

A dummy is a common comforter for young children. As they grow older they are more likely to use a piece of soft material which they may become very attached to. Comforters are useful in the development of independence and learning to feel secure, but they can get in the way of everyday life if using one becomes stuck as a habit and the child become dependent on it, rather than learning to become self-reliant.

When should you worry about your child's comforter and try and remove it? Unfortunately there is no easy answer to this, but here are some of the things that you should take into account:

- After the age of three to four years old, comforters will begin to get in the way of the normal development of independence.
- Older children who use comforters in public are likely to be teased.
- A comforter can become too important for a child so that he or she becomes very distressed if it isn't immediately available.
- It is best to remove a comforter gradually rather than do it suddenly.

- Children who are distressed for a good reason may benefit from a comforter, so don't remove it until they are more settled.
- Even much older children and some adults may use a comforter at night without being particularly disturbed. This only means that the habit has become stuck.
- Keeping a comforter habit going may get in the way of the child growing up and may encourage the child to remain immature.

Dummies and pieces of material wear out or are lost and it is up to parents to decide whether or not to replace them. If they are replaced then the habit is obviously going to carry on. As soon as parents have agreed that the comforter habit is no longer helpful, the process can be speeded up by 'losing' the comforter for progressively longer periods and removing little pieces from it until it disappears altogether!

HEAD-BANGING

Many young children around 6–30 months hit their heads on the pillow or on the cot. This is a normal stage of development that may go on for longer in some children. It may sometimes become quite a problem, keeping the rest of the family awake with the noise or the worry about what damage the child might be doing to the head – or the house!

In order to deal with the habit of head-banging it is necessary to know why it happens in the first place. Here are some of the reasons:

- to release morphine-like substances in the brain
- lack of stimulation
- as a result of a tantrum
- as a comforting habit

- boredom
- to produce a pleasant sensation
- to gain attention.

Habits are usually kept going by several factors working together. Some of the causes of the habit seem very different from each other. For example, if children are given attention for head-banging, then it won't take them long to work out how to make people take notice of them. On the other hand if the habit is ignored it will probably carry on in spite of receiving no attention, because the head-banging habit is comforting in itself.

You can see that it is not at all easy to stop head-banging. Telling children to 'stop it' or going to the children to try and distract them usually makes it more likely to carry on because the behaviour has gained some attention.

The key to dealing with head-banging is to make sure that the least sensation and pleasure as possible is caused by it. When you think about it, it is obvious that children must get something from head-banging – strange as it may seem – otherwise why do it?

One of the problems is that the sudden stopping movement caused by head-banging has been shown to release opiate-like substances in the brain that give pleasant sensations. Also head-banging usually produces a noise that becomes comforting in the same way as listening to music is enjoyable. With these points in mind, here are some ideas about how to deal with head-banging:

- Avoid giving attention – try not to go to your child during the head-banging unless you think he or she may cause serious damage.
- Make sure that the area where the head-banging occurs is soft and can absorb the blows.
- An arrangement of pillows and foam-rubber may

help, but make sure that a young child can't eat the foam.

- Deal with boredom, lack of stimulation or tempers in the usual way.
- Make sure that the bed doesn't make a creaking sound and try and reduce the noise caused to the minimum.
- If all else fails, putting the mattress on the floor in the middle of the room (away from all potential 'banging surfaces') usually works for night-time head-banging and rocking.

Of course it isn't that easy to ignore a child who is head-banging when the whole house is rattling with the crashing vibration! Fortunately it is very unusual for children to do any damage as a result of the banging. Most children know just how hard to bang. A slight bruise does no harm, but if you think that the eyes may be in danger or the bruise produces a large, raised bump, it is advisable to have professional advice.

If you decide to put a mattress on the floor, you may also have to think about other furniture that your child might use to bang on and find a way of making the room safe with as few noisy bits and hard edges as possible. Make sure that your child is warm enough and quite safe so that you won't have to go into the room when the head-banging starts.

Head-banging in temper can be dealt with in much the same way. You need to be sure that the child is safe and then leave your child to calm down, knowing that tantrums only occur in front of an audience. Head-banging children realize that they will have an audience because the noise will be heard throughout the house and is very difficult to ignore (see my book *Bad Behaviour, Tantrums and Tempers* in this series.)

ROCKING

Rocking is very similar to head-banging in all respects, but because it causes less noise and no damage it is easier to ignore. But simply ignoring rocking may not be enough to stop it. The habit is pleasant enough in itself to keep it going and the longer it goes on, the more likely it is to continue.

The natural response to a child who is rocking is to do something to stop it, but just like head-banging, paying any attention at all to the rocking will actually make it more likely to occur again. Putting the mattress on the floor is helpful for children who rock in bed. Most beds move and squeak with the rocking which only increases the sensations and interest in keeping it going.

One method that has been used for rocking is to use a rhythmical sound like a metronome that is set to go at a rate that is a bit faster or slower than the child can rock. The idea is that this will put the child off. You will have to experiment with the speed.

Unless there is some underlying problem that is maintaining the rocking, you can expect children to grow out of it eventually and because it causes no harm there is no point in worrying about it. If you have done all the things I have outlined above, you have done all you can.

Usually these approaches can be expected to show an improvement within a few days. But they need to be continued for at least six weeks before giving up. They can always be tried again later if the habit remains or returns. Children tend to rock more if they are distressed and upset about anything. So if your child's rocking doesn't respond to the usual methods of coping you should think about what might be upsetting your child and then deal with it.

NAIL-BITING AND FINGER-PICKING

Thumb-sucking is sometimes replaced by nail-biting which, once established, may continue on well into adult life. In fact 'hand to mouth' habits are very common in adults and can usually be traced back to childhood. This is one of the reasons why parents are keen to try and stop nail-biting. Unfortunately, nail-biting is almost as difficult to stop as smoking. The person has to be very keen to stop doing it otherwise it is likely to carry on.

The trouble is that nails and fingers are always available for biting or picking at any moment of the day or night. They are familiar and friendly and therefore difficult to refuse! It all happens automatically and unconsciously, so there is no point in blaming the nail-biters – they can't help it.

Fussing and going on to about how bad nail-biting is will only make it worse. In fact almost anything that you do to stop it is likely to have the opposite effect. It doesn't sound easy to deal with, does it? However, here are a few ideas that you can try that should help:

- Most important is to help your child to want to stop biting and picking, to want to look after the nails and let them grow properly.
- Putting bitter aloes or some other unpleasant tasting substance on the nails doesn't usually work but may help as a reminder if your child is well motivated to stop.
- Marking the fingers in some way such as with a dot of nail varnish may serve as a reminder not to bite them.
- Wrapping the nails in a little sticky plaster can help the less well-motivated child to remember not to bite.
- Finding any way to allow even one nail to grow properly may help to stop the habit.

- Teaching the child when the 'at risk' times are for nail-biting together with a method of keeping the nails out of harm's way will train your child to learn how to stop the habit by his or her own efforts.

A child nail-biting in public can easily embarrass parents and make them want to say 'for goodness sake stop biting your ***** nails.' Unfortunately this only works for a minute or two and in the long run makes it more likely that the nail-biting will continue. The best way of dealing with nail-biting in public is any one of these three approaches:

1. Find something that keeps the hands busy doing something else – 'just hold this for me please,' without mentioning the nail-biting at all.
2. If all else fails it is better to reach out casually and gently but firmly remove the fingers from the mouth with out saying a word. While you are doing this just carry on with whatever you were doing and don't even look at your child.
3. Do nothing at all. Make a mental note that you will have to find a way of helping your child to be more keen to stop nail-biting.

NOSE-WIPING AND -PICKING

Nose-picking is a good example of how a very normal and understandable behaviour can become embarrassing and even antisocial if it becomes a regular habit. As with all other habits, telling your child to 'stop it' is more likely to have the opposite effect in the long run and increase the frequency of picking. But ignoring it will only allow the nose-picking to continue.

Although using the back of the hand or the sleeve to dry a

drippy nose is the normal method used by young children, it isn't a pretty sight. Most parents can't resist saying 'don't do that dear,' but with little effect. The dripping nose is a good example of where it is best to get in first with a good habit before a bad one becomes fixed. This won't stop nose-picking or -wiping, but it will make either much less likely to becomes stuck as a habit.

Here are some ways of encouraging some good 'nose habits' early on so that 'finger up the nose habits' can be prevented:

- Try and make sure that the nose is dry and clean until your child is able to do this alone.
- Teach your child how to use a hanky — in every detail.
- Make sure that there is always a hanky available.
- Remind your child to wipe the nose with a hanky if it needs it.
- Keep this routine going until you are quite confident that your child has the clean, dry nose habit firmly fixed.

You will probably be thinking 'that all seems common sense — what is so special about that?' Nothing really, except that most parents don't do it, which is why so many children use fingers and sleeves to keep their noses clean. Children need much more teaching on how to blow their noses and keep them clean than might be expected.

Many parents prefer tissues to hankies, but they are not without problems. Tissues quickly become soggy and disintegrate and it is difficult to keep enough of them to hand. I think hankies are better for children to learn on. However, even with all the best teaching, some children still manage to have nose-picking and -wiping habits.

Here are some things that you can do if your child has a bad nose-picking habit:

- Every time that the child uses a finger or sleeve, immediately ask for an action replay, but done correctly with a hanky this time.
- Avoid making it into a big issue.
- Repeat the teaching of how to look after the nose properly.
- Ask 'do you need a hanky?' as a way of reminding your child what he or she should be doing.
- Offer a hanky rather than saying 'stop picking.'

Nose habits are of course more frequent in the winter, but they are also more common if a child hasn't got easy access to a hanky or if the child has hay fever. Allergies that affect the lining of the nose not only make the nose run more but they also make it itchy. Your GP will be able to help in diagnosing allergic rhinitis. However, apart from a frequently blocked or runny nose, a typical sign is a horizontal crease half way up the nose due to repeatedly wiping it with the back of the hand or sleeve.

If you have tried all the things I have mentioned above without much success, then it is likely that there is some irritation keeping the habit going. The following points are worth considering:

- A nasal allergy causing irritation and discharge may need specific treatment.
- A dry or polluted atmosphere can cause the nose to itch.
- Dry crusts in the nose cause irritation. They can be softened with a mild antiseptic ointment or vaseline.
- Repeated fiddling with the nose may itself encourage infection and itching. Any skin infection around the nose will need to be treated.

Nose-picking and -wiping cause strong reactions in other people, but do try and avoid becoming emotional about it. It isn't that serious and if you follow the guidelines above, quietly and calmly, the habit can be expected to settle down eventually. But don't expect too much success before your child is 8–10 years old.

SNIFFING

Some children learn to sniff as an alternative to wiping the nose with the back of the hand. Unfortunately the repeated sniffing noise can become quite annoying for some people. A sniffing habit is much more likely to occur if there is any cause for irritation of the nose (as described above) and this needs to be dealt with if possible.

The problem with sniffing is that we all do it and it is mainly a question of how loud is 'acceptable' for a sniff. Because it is so much a matter of opinion and not an 'all or nothing' behaviour, sniffing habits can be difficult to deal with. However, here are some ideas:

- Make sure that there is no persistent nasal irritation.
- Make sure that the sniffer always has a hanky.
- Avoid saying 'stop it.'
- Avoid getting worked up about it.
- Ask the child to use a hanky or tissue instead of sniffing.
- Say 'please use your hanky' if your child sniffs too loudly.

In some cases the sniffing can become so fixed that it becomes part of a tic, when it is usually associated with a twitch of the nose and face as well (see Chapter 4, 'Twitches and Tics'). If the sniffing has not improved in spite of all your efforts, try not to become upset – it only makes things worse. If the sniffing is winding you up and making you feel irritable and upset, then it is advisable to find some way of shutting the sound out, for example, by talking a lot, using a personal stereo or simply going to another room.

SKIN-PICKING AND SCRATCHING

Habits that involve the skin almost always start off with some form of itch or soreness. Scratching makes it feel better, only for the itch to become worse again soon afterwards – leading to another scratch. This quickly becomes a vicious circle and before long the scratching or skin-picking continues out of habit and for no other reason. This type of habit is much more likely to occur if there is something already wrong with the skin, such as:

- eczema
- spots and pimples
- cuts and grazes
- any itchy condition.

All the general rules about habits apply to skin habits. But the skin does have one advantage – it can be covered over with plaster or a bandage to stop the fingers getting at it. This will deal with most scratching and picking habits, but not so easily with widespread conditions such as eczema. Here are some strategies you can try:

- Deal with the cause of any irritation.
- Ask for medical advice if the irritation continues.
- Keep the scratched area covered during periods when scratching is most likely to occur – night-time is usually the worst time.
- Sometimes, just putting some cream on the scratched

skin may act as a reminder not to do it again.
- Cut the finger-nails short and file them daily.
- Try and keep the hands busy doing other things.
- It may help to offer a small reward for not scratching or picking – as measured by the appearance of the skin.

Sometimes the scratching habit continues in spite of everything, with the skin showing all the signs of being picked and scratched but with the child denying all scratching and never being seen doing it. The usual explanation for this mystery is that the child is either doing it when alone and unobserved or when asleep – or both.

LIP-LICKING

A sore red ring around the lips isn't unusual in young children, especially in the winter. This habit starts with dry or sore lips that are licked frequently. This in turn makes the skin around the lips wet and more likely to become sore so that a licking habit soon develops. If this carries on for long enough the skin can easily become infected, so medical advice is needed.

If there is no skin infection, then it may help to use a simple ointment such as vaseline to cover the red skin – especially when going outside in the wind and the cold. The ointment must of course be safe to be licked and swallowed and care must be taken that the ointment doesn't make the rash worse – if so, get specialist advice.

All the other general points about dealing with habits should be considered, but lip-licking can be very difficult to deal with and you may have to wait for the summer before the lips improve.

THE HABIT THAT WILL NOT STOP

These common habits can be very difficult to stop once they have become fixed. Some children are much more likely than others to become stuck in habits and if one habit does eventually fade, it may soon be replaced by another one. Here are some other reasons why a child may have a habit that is unusually difficult to stop:

- The habit has gone on for a year or more.
- The child enjoys the habit or the reaction it causes.
- Only half-hearted efforts have been made to stop it.
- People have given up trying to stop it too soon.
- The child has an underlying emotional problem.
- The child is unmotivated to stop the habit.
- The child has an underlying physical problem.

It is always possible that a habit may come to serve some other purpose such as gaining attention or distracting parents from other worries. In which case the habit may continue in spite of all efforts to stop it.

Fortunately, most habits have no deep hidden purpose or meaning and are not a sign of disturbance in the child or the family.

In the rare cases where the habit is part of a more extensive disturbance it will usually be obvious what the underlying problem is. But even in these cases it is worthwhile having a go at stopping the habit using the guidelines above. It will often be successful and at least that will be one less problem to worry about.

CONCLUSION

Most children go through a period of having a simple but neverthess rather annoying habit. They usually fade away of their own accord, but these habits can be socially disabling and are best stopped if at all possible. There are many things that can be done to stop habits. The principles are the same. Prevention of the habit is the main approach, while at the same time encouraging your child to do whatever possible to stop the habit. The art is to be able to avoid all emotional upset about the habit. Easier said than done sometimes! But if you persevere, you should succeed in getting your child to kick the habit.

3

. . . . .

Sleep and Night-time Habits

Many of our daily habits are concentrated around preparing for bed, going to sleep and getting up in the morning. This is not that surprising because these are times of change where regular routines can make life much easier and reduce some of the anxiety and feelings of insecurity that so often accompany any change. Some of these night-time habits and rituals have already been described in Chapter 1.

A good sleep habit is one of the first regular routines that children get into. But about one in three infants and young children up to the age of five years old are reported to have disturbed sleep and of these about 30 per cent could be regarded as having a serious problem. Fortunately, as children grow older, this high rate of disturbed sleep improves and by eight years old the frequency of sleep problems is down to one in 10.

So many children are affected and yet so few parents are sure about what they should do about sleep problems that they have almost reached epidemic proportions. Why should this be? Here are some possible explanations:

- Few families have regular bedtime routines.
- Over-tired parents find it difficult to be firm and consistent.
- Parental guilt feelings lead to over-indulgence.
- Childcare experts, GPs, friends and relatives give contradictory advice.

NORMAL SLEEP HABITS

The new-born infant spends the majority of the day and night asleep, but is only asleep for relatively short periods of about 20 minutes. This means that babies wake up naturally every 20 minutes or so, but if contented and undisturbed they will probably drift back into a further period of sleep. So it is normal for babies to wake and cry very frequently.

By three months old, children spend more time awake during the day than during the night, but there are still four to five periods of wakefulness during the night when the child may be quiet or may cry. Later on, around the age of six months, most children spend a reasonably long time asleep during the night (up to 15 hours) and a clear day/night sleep pattern is normally established. For this reason it is best to wait until at least six months of age before taking any action to deal with a child's disturbed sleep pattern.

At six months old most children have settled into a reasonably stable sleep/waking cycle, but by two years this has often broken down, especially if a regular sleep routine has not been firmly established. Sleep, just like eating, toileting and dressing is a daily habit that requires regular training before it becomes properly established. There are several different factors that make children more likely to be wakeful at night. These include the following:

- temperament (children with strong emotions and poor adaptability to change are more likely to have sleep difficulties)
- birth difficulties and irritable babies with colic
- parental worries and anxiety
- feeding at night after one year of age
- sleeping in the same room as the parents
- over-responsive parents.

45

There is some evidence that children sleep less now than they did in the first part of this century. However, if children are put to bed early enough and left undisturbed, the difference disappears. It seems that our present-day lifestyle provides less opportunity for children to sleep than was the case when their grandparents were children!

WHY WORRY ABOUT SLEEP?

Some people believe that there is no need to worry about children's sleep because they will eventually make it up naturally if you leave them alone and stop worrying about it. On the other hand, there is evidence that sleep deprivation has a bad effect on children – as well as on their parents.

Lack of sleep leads to poor concentration and irritability (after 24 hours of wakefulness), followed by anxiety and feelings of depression (after 48 hours). These effects are shared by both children and adults. But there is one big difference between children and adults: as children become more tired, they tend to speed up, becoming restless and apparently energetic, whereas most adults slow down and run out of energy.

The combination of a tired and irritable parent with a restless, sleepless child is not a happy one. But this is not the only problem caused by the wakeful child. Parents need time for themselves. Time to communicate and to enjoy being together. A sleepless child can make this very difficult.

In spite of the obvious need for sleep, there is no way that sleep can be actually forced on a child. Indeed, telling children to go to sleep usually wakes them up! So don't bother to try and control your child's sleep. All you can do is to make sure that your child has the right conditions for sleep. In other words, that the child is lying comfortably in bed in a quiet, darkened room. There is some evidence that just resting in bed at night is almost as good for you as sleep itself.

THE WAKEFUL CHILD –
ARE THERE EASY SOLUTIONS?

Most parents will try anything to lull their wakeful child off to sleep. Reassuring words, rearranging the bed clothes, stroking, rocking or giving a cuddle are the usual methods. More desperate solutions involve walking the child around the streets in the middle of the night or going for a drive in the car. If all else fails, the child is taken into the parents' bed or someone moves in with the child. Easy and effective – the crying stops and eventually the child goes off to sleep. But what is the cost?

Children are quick to realize that by staying awake and calling out they can control their parents and obtain lots of extra attention and cuddles. It only takes a few months for children to work this one out. In fact, children are often better at training their parents into a night-time routine than the other way round!

Sedative drugs are another apparently easy way of dealing with the wakeful child. If the dose is large enough it can be guaranteed to work. However, most sedative drugs are not effective for more than four hours – unless they are given in such large doses that the side-effects of drowsiness and irritability remain present during the next day. A rebound increase in disturbed sleep may make it difficult to stop the drug and the underlying sleep problems still remain to be dealt with.

These quick and easy solutions can be effective in the short term, but they have a cost. Rather like a bank overdraft – it feels good at the time, but there is a payment to be made later! Eventually the child has to be weaned off the drug or got out of the parents' bed. Otherwise they may become permanently dependent on the drug – or on someone else to be with them to help them off to sleep.

The only time that drugs might be justified is during a crisis, when the time limit for medication should be three to four days. Any longer than this and alternative approaches should be used.

NIGHT-TIME IS FOR SLEEPING AND...

There is more to night-time than just sleeping. Resting is also important and parents also need to have some peace and quiet and some time for themselves.

Less obviously, night-time is when children can begin to learn to feel confident on their own, without being dependent on anyone else. Night-time is one of the very few occasions when children are completely alone for any length of time (in their own bed, quiet and self-contained, even if other siblings are in the same room with them) and therefore able to learn to be comfortable on their own and develop self-reliance.

The process of becoming self-reliant and developing some independence seems to be more urgent these days, as young children are expected to cope with the world outside the family at a much earlier age even than was the case a generation ago. Being able to feel safe and self-contained in the dark during the night helps to develop the confidence that all children need to cope with new experiences, for example when starting school.

So you can see that night-time is for sleeping and...

- rest and recovery (just lying in bed is enough)
- peace and quiet for parents
- time for parents to do what they want on their own
- a time to learn to cope with being alone
- an opportunity to develop self-confidence
- learning to cope in the dark.

PREPARING FOR BED

The importance of a regular bedtime routine can't be stressed enough. One of the main reasons why sleep programmes don't work is that insufficient effort is put into getting the bedtime routine well established. The following approach is recommended:

- Take time to work out a detailed routine that suits your family.
- Start the routine one hour before bedtime.
- It may help to write it all down.
- Agree a bedtime that can be kept to.
- Gradually wind things down.
- Always do the same things in the same order.
- Once your child is in bed, spend only a short time with your child – unless there are very good reasons for staying longer. Children obviously need more individual time than this, but it is usually better to spend it with them at some other time during the day.
- Always say exactly the same words when saying good-night.
- Turn the light out and shut the bedroom door.

This routine needs some explanation. It is important that the bedtime is not fixed too late. Parents often allow their children to dictate a late bedtime and justify it by claiming 'He won't sleep if we put him to bed earlier.' Don't forget that night-time is for resting as well as sleeping, so it isn't a big deal if a child lies awake.

The winding-down period gives the child a signal that bedtime is approaching without the need to get into an argument about it. Here are some of the steps in the winding-down routine that you could use:

- Turn the TV off.
- Play only quiet games.
- Use the clock.
- Draw the curtains.
- Turn down the lights.
- Playing some quiet, relaxing music may help.

Using the clock can be very helpful because it can't be argued with. A sticker on the clock face can help to reinforce the timing of the routine. If necessary set an alarm or timer that will let everyone know that bedtime has come.

It is important that parents agree on bedtimes for their children and choose one that suits them rather than fits in with their child's demands. The following bedtimes are reasonable guidelines to follow if you are not quite sure what to do or if you can't agree about the time:

- Under 3 years – before 6 o'clock
- Under 5 – before 7
- Under 7 – before 7.30
- Under 10 – before 8.00
- Under 13 – before 8.30
- Under 15 – before 9.00.

You may think these time are very early, but they are not unreasonable. The advantage of having slightly early bedtimes is that it gives you the possibility of generously allowing your child to stay up later on special occasions without it being too late.

LEAVING THE BEDROOM

Once your child is in bed, the longer you stay in the bedroom the more likely it is that the child will complain when you do eventually leave the room. A short story, a prayer or a lullaby and a cuddle is all that is needed before saying the same good-night phrase such as: 'Good-night, God bless, see you in the morning.' The repetition of the same phrase will eventually come to signal automatically that it is time for sleep – almost like hypnotic suggestion. The same 'good-night phrase' can then be used at other times during the night if, for example, a child is woken by a bad dream or is ill in the night.

It helps children to get used to having the light off and the door shut during the night because darkness and quietness prepares the brain for sleep. Leaving a night-light on and keeping the bedroom door open gives children the wrong message:

- that the darkness is dangerous
- that parents have no confidence in their child being able to cope alone
- that it is time for playing – not sleeping
- that the open door is an invitation to come out.

That is the theory, but many parents have been afraid of the dark themselves and may still prefer to sleep with the light on or the door open. Parents will need to decide how they would like their child to cope in the dark. Parents who would like the door shut but also wish to be able to look into the room to check that all is well could try any of the following suggestions:

- Leave the door ajar, but not wide enough for the child to get through.
- Put a mirror or glass-fronted picture on the wall so that a reflection of the child's bed can be seen without opening the door further.
- Place the bed in such a way that it can be seen without having to open the door much.
- Use a baby alarm and switch it on whenever necessary to check that all is well.
- Put a peep hole in the door!

Making these special arrangements may seem rather silly, but there are obvious advantages in being able to check your child without having to go into the bedroom while the child is still awake or only lightly asleep.

NOW THE DIFFICULT BIT!

Most parents can manage to get their children to bed, but if this isn't possible then there is a rather serious disciplinary problem and there are likely to be other disciplinary difficulties during the day as well (see my book *Bad Behaviour, Tantrums and Tempers* in this series for help with discipline). However, the more usual difficulty is finding a way to *keep* the child quietly in bed. This is also largely a question of discipline.

A child has to be actually taught to stay in bed – or at least in the bedroom. Of course, if the child is still in a cot there is no problem – if the child has taken to climbing out of the cot, it's time to get a bed!

When the child is in a normal bed, some parents may use a lock on the bedroom door or a stair gate in the doorway. However, it is best to avoid a real lock on the bedroom door in favour of a 'psychological' lock where a child knows for certain that he or she isn't allowed to go wandering around the house at night and must stay in the bedroom. Except, of course, to go to the toilet or if there were an emergency.

The quickest way of achieving a 'psychological lock' on the bedroom door is to catch the child at the earliest possible moment after getting out of bed. If the wakeful child is able to wander around or get into the parents' bed without anyone knowing, this behaviour is very likely to continue.

A very clear message to stay in bed must be given to the wandering child. You will have to practise giving this message until it has the effect that you want. Here are some of the ways you can make sure that your instructions are clear:

- Put on your serious expression.
- Use a commanding tone of voice.
- Give a firm gesture – pointing to the bed.
- Show a determined look in your eyes.
- Use as few words as possible.

Try saying 'stay in bed' in front of the mirror or to another adult to see if your performance is any good. You will have to be able to put on an impressive performance – just like being an actor or actress – otherwise your child will take no notice. In the end it is your child who will let you know how impressive your performance is. For most children only an Oscar-winning show will do!

If your child takes little or no notice, more practice is obviously needed to improve your performance. At this stage it is important to keep going and not to give up. If it isn't possible to control a small child enough to stop in the bedroom, there could also be a problem in situations that are potentially dangerous, such as running into the street or putting a hand too near the fire.

The Next Difficult Bit

Assuming that you have been successful in keeping the child in the bedroom, the next problem is that the child will soon start to call out to attract you back into the room. The reasons for calling out are endless:

- I am thirsty.
- I want to go to the toilet.
- I can't sleep.
- I am hungry.
- I have a head/tummy/leg ache.
- I am too hot/too cold.

- Mummy!...Daddy!
- I am scared of...

If you wish help your child to get into a good sleep habit, you will have to resist answering these calls and make sure that no one else responds either. The more you meet the demands, the more demands will be made. This means not going into the bedroom and not answering the call at all – *provided that you are confident that your child is not ill or in any danger*. This will mean going against your natural instinct. Refusing to respond to your child's demands won't be easy.

It is only reasonable to refuse to respond to children's demands and insist that they remain in the bedroom if you are absolutely sure that –

1. *The bedroom is completely safe for children.* The windows must be child-proof and there must be nothing in the room that children can climb on in a dangerous way or pull down on top of themselves.
2. *The child is not ill or in any discomfort.*

Parents will know if their children are ill or in discomfort from the way in which they cry and from their behaviour. Assuming that you are sure that your child is indeed safe and well and that you have been successful in getting the message across that the child must stay in the bedroom, then you must stay out of the bedroom even if your child makes very heavy demands that you come in. Here are some of the things that children try in order to get their parents to come to them:

- crying
- screaming
- head-banging
- breath-holding
- vomiting.

Bedwetting may also occur, but does not need to have anything done about it until the morning. Remember that tens of thousands of children wet their beds each night without being changed until the next morning.

Head-banging usually stops if parents take no notice. But if it continues, some sponge-rubber protection may help. The aim is to limit the sensory stimulation that the head-banging produces – the noise and the attention, for instance. One easy and effective solution for head-banging is to put the child to sleep on a mattress on the floor.

Breath-holding following screaming tempers can be frightening but does no harm and always resolves itself spontaneously. So it is best to allow the child to cope with it alone. An audience will make all these behaviours more likely to recur.

Being sick is the ultimate weapon that some children use in order to get their parents' attention and to make sure that their demands are met. It usually occurs after a screaming temper has gone on for a while and the child has become frenzied. If parents wish to go into the room to clear up the vomit, it should be done quickly with the minimum of fuss and attention (e.g. take two towels into the room. Use one to wipe up the vomit and the other to put over the damp patch. Then leave the room without saying a word or looking the child in the face. It is better to say nothing if your child has been sick deliberately).

It is easy to think that the distressed state that young children get themselves into must be damaging. However,there is no evidence that this form of attention-seeking screaming does any harm at all to young children. Quite the reverse is the case. Trying to soothe a child in this state generally makes it more likely to recur. But it is only reasonable to leave a child to cry and scream if the parents are sure that their child is **not** ill and that the bedroom is completely safe, using the following check-list:

Is the child safe?

1. Was the child well on being put to bed?
2. Has the child got a temperature? – If unsure, use a thermometer.
3. Is the child warm enough? – An all-in-one sleep suit may help.

Is the room safe?

1. Can the child fall out of bed? – Put the mattress on the floor.
2. Could any furniture fall over? – Fix it to the wall.
3. Is the window safe? – Use child-proof locks.

All this may seem a little over-dramatic. However, it helps to go through the worst possible scenario that could happen so that you can feel able to cope with any eventuality and therefore feel more confident.

Some parents will feel that they are unable to stand the crying and obvious distress of their child. In this case there is another approach that is described later. However, you can see that there are potential problems if children are able to ignore your instructions and do what they want or if they learn that they can get their wishes met just by being difficult and demanding.

The main worry that parents have is that their children may become very anxious and disturbed if left alone at night without reassurance. On the other hand children have to learn how to cope with their own fears and worries and can only do this by facing up to them on their own (see my book *Worries and Fears* in this series).

It may seem a hard lesson to teach children that they have to learn to cope alone sometimes and can't have every wish or need met immediately, but it is far better to teach them this early on, before they start school. Certainly by the time a child has reached adolescence it is too late. Fortunately there is considerable evidence that being firm about something you know is best for your child will be helpful even if some distress is caused.

A THREE-NIGHT GUARANTEE

If the sleep programme outlined above is followed to the letter, at least an 80 per cent improvement can be expected within three nights. Many parents will say that they have done it before and it hasn't worked, but when they go over it in detail they find that they have not really carried it through completely. Either the child has been allowed out of the bedroom or the parents have responded in some way to the crying.

The difficulty of keeping to this sleep programme should not be underestimated and it will often be necessary to have intensive support from a trusted friend or relative to help you to stick to the programme. It is important to remember that if you do decide to use this approach *it needs to be followed through*. If you stop half-way through, you may be worse off than when you started.

In the end, each set of parents has to decide how important it is for their child to have a good sleep habit and to be able to remain alone at night. You may feel that it is not worth all the hassle. If this is how you feel, don't worry, there are many other parents who feel just the same. Japanese parents, for example, often allow their children to sleep in bed with them until they reach puberty. However, their family system is generally very close-knit.

IT DIDN'T WORK FOR ME

It can be expected that some of you will by now be thinking 'I have tried this and it didn't work for me.' If so, there must have been some loop-hole that was allowed to creep into the programme. Try and identify these weak areas before trying again. Here is a check-list you can use if you would like to be successful next time:

- *Who gave in first?* This person will need to be persuaded that it is all right to be firm and that it will do the child no harm to stay alone in bed and to cry for attention. This person will also need a lot of support and comfort during this difficult time.
- *What is the worst thing that could happen?* Work this out beforehand and prepare for it in advance.
- *Who can give additional support?* It helps to have someone outside the family who has confidence in this approach and has used it successfully before.
- *Will any relative or friend undermine the programme?* Grannies and neighbours are often good at sabotaging!
- *How will you cope after many hours of screaming?* It is best to start the new sleep routine at a time when you can afford to be tired the next day. If you start on Friday night, the sleep routine should be working by Monday!
- *Will somebody be able to look after you and all the strong feelings that you can expect to have?* Parents must work together on the routine and agree to look after each other. This is more difficult if you are a single parent, but hopefully you should be able to find someone who is prepared to give you support over this time.

It is quite common for parents to give all kinds of reasons for not being able to follow the programme through, such as:

- *My neighbours will complain about the screaming.* Warn them beforehand and explain that it will only last two to three nights.
- *Somebody might call the Social Services if they hear the screaming.* Explain (to anyone who might be disturbed by the noise) what you are doing – and show them this chapter!
- *My child's brothers and sisters may be kept awake by the crying.* Most children sleep through all kinds of noise, but if there is a problem, send the other children away to sleep with friends or relatives for two to three nights.
- *I can't afford to go without sleep.* Start the sleep programme at the weekend or during holiday time.
- *We disagree and are not fully motivated.* Wait until you are ready to tackle the problem together.

The sleep habit training programme will be much more difficult to apply to children as they grow older. Children aged eight and older will probably need specialist help if they still have a poor sleep habit. By this time the approach described above will probably be impossible to follow through because the child will have grown too big and too demanding. Other techniques such as teaching relaxation for the child and special help for the parents may be necessary. The alternative approach described below may be a better option for older children.

AN ALTERNATIVE APPROACH

Some parents will find this 'in at the deep end' approach too demanding to manage. Apart from the 'easy options' described above, there is another approach that is often recommended. The first part of the bedtime routine is just the same, but with this method the parent spends progressively less time in the child's bedroom each night, following a carefully worked out schedule, as follows:

1. Decide how long it is necessary for you to stay in your child's room.
2. Reduce this time each night by a set number of minutes.
3. Stick strictly to this timetable.
4. It may help to use a chart to record progress and to have small rewards for progress.

The problem with this type of graduated programme is that all may go well for several nights, but when children realize what is happening, they often become even more difficult and demanding and everything will slip back to square one.

THE BIG PAY-OFF

None of the crying or screaming would be worth all the emotional stress unless a reasonable pay-off could be expected. Fortunately there is something in it for everyone – even the neighbours!

Advantages for the child

- more rested
- less irritable and hyperactive
- less disobedient
- more self-reliant

Advantages for the parents

- more time for themselves
- more confidence in managing the child
- more rest and sleep

Advantages for other children, neighbours, etc.

- less disturbance at night
- less tired during the day

When parents have been successful in establishing a good sleep habit they invariably feel more competent and confident. They agree that the short-term distress was certainly worthwhile. The only feeling of regret that some parents have is that they did not follow the programme right through before.

In the end it is for parents to decide what is best for their own child. But parents should know that if they are unable to establish a regular bedtime and sleep routine they can expect some or all of the following problems as their child grows older:

- continuing disturbed nights
- increasing family stress
- immature behaviour
- relatively high dependency
- problems with discipline.

In spite of the positive effects of the approach I have described above, there will always be a few people who are against causing any distress to a child, fearing that it must inevitably lead to long-term psychological harm later on in adult life. There is no evidence to support this view, which makes the assumption that distress can somehow be avoided in life. In fact there is evidence that carefully measured and controlled distress can have a positive and protective effect on children, making them more resilient and psychologically healthy.

CONCLUSION

From the age of six months it should be possible to train a child into a good sleep habit, no matter how disabled or disturbed the child is. The process of establishing a night-time routine and a regular sleep pattern is central to basic childcare. Success in establishing a good night-time routine leads to increased confidence and happiness all round, making all the hard work well worth the effort.

4

· · · · ·

Twitches and Tics

Many children go through a phase when they have an uncontrollable twitch or tic. This usually occurs between the ages of two and 15 years, but the most common time for tics is five to nine years of age. Tics generally fade away on their own accord and in many cases the twitches are not that obvious and may only last for a few weeks. However, about 15 per cent of children go through a longer phase lasting months or years, during which they have tics that cause some problem.

Tics tend to change as time passes. A child may start with blinking then go on to twitching the face and then grunting. Tics are not quite the same as habits because they are:

- repeated more frequently
- more difficult to control by will-power
- more rapid in movement
- distressing to the child
- without purpose
- more common in boys
- more simple and uncomplicated.

In spite of these differences, tics are similar to habits in that they are *not* caused by insecurity or emotional disorder. However, both tics and habits are likely to be made worse and therefore to be more noticeable when children are:

- emotionally upset or insecure
- bored or under-stimulated
- excited or over-stimulated.

Anything that unsettles the balance of emotions and stimulation of the body or mind can alter the rate at which tics occur and how severe they are. But this is not the cause of tics. In fact almost any condition including everyday habits like nail-biting are affected in the same way. Tics and habits are therefore made worse by boredom and excitement as well as by feelings of distress.

WHAT CAUSES TICS?

Because tics are so obvious and make children look different from normal, it is easy to assume that there must be something very wrong with the child and that there should be some deep underlying disturbance of the emotions. But because so many children go through a phase of twitching, it suggests that only very slight variations from normal can cause the problem of tics.

The most recent evidence suggests that tics are due to the chemical and nerve structure of the brain being slightly out of balance. In other words, the main cause of tics is physical. Here is some of the evidence that supports the view that tics are caused by the physical make-up of a child:

- Tics occur most frequently at a particular stage of brain development.
- Tics are more common in boys than in girls.
- Tics are often associated with hyperactivity and restlessness.
- Most children grow out of tics as they grow older and the brain matures.

- Drugs that affect the brain chemicals are the most effective treatment.
- There is evidence of a genetic factor – other family members may also be affected.

One way of understanding that only a very slight alteration in the balance of the nerves and chemicals in normal brain development could cause such an obvious disturbance as a tic, is to think of a TV set that is slightly out of adjustment. If the horizontal hold on the TV is only a little out of tune, the picture will 'twitch' occasionally, but only the smallest adjustment of the controls will make the picture steady again.

UNDERSTANDING TICS

There is some evidence that tics are based on the 'startle response' that is present from birth but gradually changes as children grow up. The startle response is the reaction that we all make to a sudden and unexpected noise or surprise – such as somebody unexpectedly jumping out from behind a door to give you a shock. The startle response is an inborn, automatic reflex that protects us from danger. Although some people startle more easily than others, it is impossible to avoid the reaction.

Children with tics have the same difficulty in controlling their twitches as somebody reacting to being startled. With total concentration it is possible to stop the tic but as soon as the child thinks about something else the tic will start again. Children do not put on tics deliberately just to annoy their parents. In fact it is very difficult to keep a tic going on purpose for more than a few minutes. Children who twitch and have tics can't help it – no more than you can avoid reacting if you are startled.

Try and imagine being startled and you will realize that with a slight shock you just blink your eyes, but with a severe startle your whole body may jump and you are also likely to shout out or swear. There is a steady progression of reactions to being startled that matches how common a particular type of tic is:

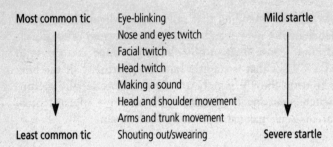

Most common tic	Eye-blinking	Mild startle
	Nose and eyes twitch	
	Facial twitch	
	Head twitch	
	Making a sound	
	Head and shoulder movement	
	Arms and trunk movement	
Least common tic	Shouting out/swearing	Severe startle

You can see that there is a very close relationship between tics and the startle response, with eye-blinking being the most common and shouting out the least common. Most children with tics have very mild twitches of the eyes and face, but with more severe tics there may also be a grunting or clicking sound in the throat as well.

The full-blown tic with strong movements of the head and shoulders together with shouting out and possibly swearing as well is called Tourette syndrome after the French doctor who first described the condition over a hundred years ago. It is rare and needs the help of a specialist.

In the same way that no one can avoid reacting to being startled, so a child with a tic has virtually no control over it. This is important to understand because parents often feel that children are deliberately twitching and could stop if they wanted to.

Tics are automatic, involuntary reactions that occur unconsciously in much the same way as sneezing with hay fever. And just like trying to avoid sneezing, it is possible to stop a tic for a while but the effort required to stop the tics is too much to keep going for very long.

Telling children to stop twitching is like telling a child with hay fever to stop sneezing. The pressure to sneeze builds up if they try and stop it until sooner or later the sneeze explodes out. Fortunately, when children are deeply asleep the tics disappear – as does the sneezing!

HOW TO COPE WITH TICS

Parents who seek help for their child's tic are usually told to ignore it and that the tic will get better on its own. Although this may be true, it doesn't usually make anyone feel any better because tics can be very distressing:

- Children with tics may be teased and picked on at school.
- Tics cause embarrassment for the sufferer.
- Parents are distressed by seeing their child twitch.
- Other people may avoid a child with tics.
- People blame the child and think the tic is deliberate.
- People blame the parents for 'making' their child twitch.

Ignoring tics and twitches is not only difficult but it doesn't help the distress and embarrassment caused by tics. In fact most of the problems of a child with a twitch are due to a lack of understanding about the nature of tics. Once parents know what tics are all about it becomes easier to cope and easier to explain what is going on to other people.

Here are some guidelines that should help if your child has a tic that is causing one or more of the problems outlined above:

1. *Give an explanation of the tic.* Make sure that friends, relatives and teachers understand the main points about tics

that are covered in this chapter. It may help to lend the book to them to read for themselves. Your child should also be given a simple explanation of what is happening to him or her.

2. *Ignore the tic as much as possible.* Ignoring a tic won't make it disappear, but it will help it to fade away gradually as the brain matures. Any reaction that other people have to the tic is likely to make it go on for longer.

3. *Protect your child from distress.* Any child who has a tic will have more problems if there is any reason for being unsettled or upset. The tic can itself cause distress, but other problems causing increased emotional tension need to be dealt with as far as possible. Remember that children with tics are often teased and bullied.

4. *Try behaviour control.* There are several different ways of helping children control their twitching and sometimes this helps because it makes children feel that at least they have some control over what is happening to them. The tic then becomes less frightening and more manageable. Here are some of the approaches that can be used:

Simple control. This involves the child using will-power to stop the tics for a short period of two or three minutes. The time is then gradually built up if the child is successful at controlling the tics.

Keeping a record. Sometimes it is helpful for a child to keep a record of anything to do with the tics. For example, the longest time without a tic or the frequency of the tic in a five-minute period. The idea behind this is to help children to feel that they have a better understanding of the tics and their attention is directed away from the problems of the tic and onto the record-keeping.

Repeating the tic. Deliberately performing the tic several times sometimes helps. The idea is that if a tic can be deliberately started and stopped it must be potentially controllable and the child feels less helpless. One approach is to repeat the tic over and over so many times and at such a speed that the muscles are exhausted – a good idea in theory but not much use in practice.

The problem with all the behaviour control approaches is that they can make things worse by drawing extra attention to the tic and by making the child feel more responsible – and therefore more guilty – for the continuation of the tic.

The use of rewards for not twitching is of very little benefit because children only have very limited control over tics. So unless easy targets are set, such as no twitches over a short period, the child will fail.

5. *Get specialist help.* If all your attempts to help your child have failed and you feel that the tics are interfering with your child's life and really are a handicap, then specialist help from a paediatrician or child psychiatrist may be necessary. There are various medications that can be given that are very effective, but they all have side-effects and need expert supervision to make sure that the side-effects aren't worse than the habits.

IF ALL ELSE FAILS

Many parents find it extremely difficult to take a relaxed view about their child's tic. The tic becomes a constant reminder that something is wrong and parents often wonder if they have caused it in some way. Tension can easily build up at home and it is not unusual for a child's twitching to be much more noticeable at home – which also upsets parents. This may indeed be due to tension, but it is just as likely to be due to the child's being more relaxed at home.

It is all too easy to think 'where have I gone wrong?' or 'he is just doing it to annoy me,' even if you know that this isn't the case. Parents need to find some way of coping without becoming too tense and upset themselves, because this only makes a child's tics worse.

Perhaps the best way of surviving is to recognize the first signs of growing tension about the twitches and before you say anything or become too upset try and do one of the following:

- Look away and do something that will take your mind off the tics.
- Go and do something in another room.
- Ask your child to do something in another room for a few minutes.
- This isn't as a punishment, but to protect them from any negative feelings.

Sometimes other children or even brothers and sisters will undermine everything you are doing to ignore the twitches and keep things calm and relaxed, by calling names and teasing your child. This must be stopped absolutely immediately because it is totally unacceptable. It should be treated just as seriously as if sharp needles were being stuck in the child!

CONCLUSION

Tics are caused by the way the balance of the nerves and chemicals in the brain are organized and are made worse by too little or too much stress and stimulation. Tics are rather different from ordinary habits, but like habits they are not an indication of serious emotional disturbance. On the other hand, tics can cause a great deal of distress and it is important that everyone concerned with a child who has tics should understand what is going on and what can be done to help.

5

· · · · ·

Obsessions and Compulsions

·

UNDERSTANDING OBSESSIONS

Obsessions are a special form of habit that has gone out of control and taken over the person, who then feels an overpowering urge to repeat the obsession over and over again. Obsessions are different from habits in the following ways:

- They are performed consciously.
- They are unwanted.
- They are resisted as far as possible.
- There is a tension that can only be relieved by performing the obsession.
- There is a feeling that the obsession gives protection from worries.
- There is a fear that if the obsession isn't carried out, something terrible might happen.

An obsession is more complicated than a habit or ritual and may involve thoughts only or have an effect on a child's behaviour as well. Just to make it more complicated, an obsessional behaviour is usually called a compulsion. So there are 'obsessional thoughts' and 'compulsive behaviours'.

Severe obsessions are not very common in children, but mild versions that only last a few days or weeks occur more frequently. The peak age for these mild obsessions is between

71

six and nine years old and then, as with habits, there is often another peak in adolescence.

A good example of a mild obsession is having a tune on the brain or a repetitive thought that keeps coming into your mind. However hard you try to get rid of the thought or the tune, it keeps coming back again and again, without being invited.

WHO HAS OBSESSIONS?

Obsessions are more common in boys than in girls, but in adult life they occur more frequently in women. Some children are much more likely to experience obsessions than others and the following conditions are linked with obsessions:

- sensitive and highly strung temperament
- family history of obsessions
- stress and depression
- anxiety and phobias
- communication difficulty
- tics and habits
- left-handedness
- obsessional personality.

Most of the conditions that make children vulnerable to obsessions are outside their control. It seems likely that the main factor that predisposes children to obsessions is their constitution or physical make-up. This then reacts with stress and tension generated in the child's environment to bring on the obsessional symptoms.

The link with obsessional personality is an interesting one in that it makes children more likely to have obsessions. However, many children with obsessions don't have this type of personality, so it is a risk factor for obsessions but doesn't cause them. The obsessional personality has the following characteristics:

- perfectionism
- a preoccupation with detail
- rigid thinking
- indecisiveness
- controlled emotions
- tendency to hoard and collect
- concern about detail.

Many of these personality traits are useful, provided that they are kept under control. Many successful athletes, doctors, lawyers and other high achievers have obsessional personalities and manage to keep the undesirable features under reasonable control.

It used to be thought that obsessions were brought on by early problems with toilet training and parent-child conflicts, but it is now quite clear that there is no evidence to support this notion. On the other hand, the onset of obsessional symptoms can usually be traced to stressful circumstances in childhood that act as a trigger to release the underlying mechanism for obsessions.

The finding that drugs which affect the levels of the transmitter chemicals in the brain have an influence on obsessional symptoms supports the idea that the balance of the chemicals and nerves in the brain is altered in people with obsessions. It seems likely that any stressful event can also alter the levels of transmitter chemicals in the brain. This view fits the observed interaction between stress and a child who is already predisposed to obsessions.

The fact that there is an underlying physical cause for obsessions doesn't mean that there is nothing that can be done about them. Quite the contrary. There are many ways of helping children and the outlook is generally better for children than it is for adults with obsessions.

COMMON OBSESSIONS AND COMPULSIONS

The link between obsessions and compulsions is a close one. Obsessional thoughts may not lead to an action, but those that do are called compulsions. Obsessional thoughts are often difficult to find out about because children usually prefer to keep them secret. The following are typical examples:

Checking: 'I must check again to be sure that it is OK.'
Questioning: 'I wonder if I have done it correctly?'
Cleaning: 'I must clean it again because it might be dirty.'
Worrying: 'I worry that something terrible will happen.'
Counting: 'I must count them again, just to be sure.'

Checking

Checking obsessions are quite common and many people go through a phase of double- or triple-checking something even though there was no need to do so. An example of a checking ritual is when children repeatedly call out 'good-night' or something similar after going to bed, just to check that their parents are still there and that all is well with the world. An answering 'good-night' from the parent doesn't satisfy the child, who continues to call out. The more a parent answers, the longer the checking will continue.

Questioning

Repeatedly asking questions is a natural stage that all children go through as part of developing their language skills and it occurs most frequently between three and six years of age. Even when the answer is given, it doesn't seem that the child has heard it because the same question is asked again a few minutes later. If older children continue to ask the same questions over and over again, this may well be a sign of a developing obsession. Questions are usually repeated more frequently at times of change, for example when going out of the house, going to school or when going to bed.

Cleaning

Obsessional cleaning can involve a child in repeatedly tidying and putting things away, with each item being put in its exact place. But the most common form of cleaning obsession is related to washing. The first sign of a washing obsession is usually when a child spends a long time in the bathroom and washes things frequently and unnecessarily.

Worrying

Obsessional worries may move on from a concern that something terrible will happen to a very detailed and specific thought. Usually the worrying thoughts are concerned with death, sex or aggression, which are often so distressing and embarrassing for the child that they are kept secret. You may need to be very understanding and ask some very delicate questions in order to find out what is worrying your child. The big problem about obsessional thoughts is that they are not at all obvious and only the person with the thoughts can control them. It is difficult for anyone else to do much to help.

Counting

Counting obsessions usually involve repeating something unnecessarily for a set number of times. Each child is likely to have their own special number of times that something has to be repeated. The numbers 3, 7 and 21 are frequently used. The child feels that the number has some magical protective power to ward off danger, but sometimes it all gets out of control and children lose count of where they are in the counting ritual and have to start all over again.

HOW TO COPE WITH OBSESSIONS

One way of understanding an obsession is that it is rather like a ball rolling down a steep hill. It won't stop on its own — something very definite has to be done if you want to bring it to a halt. Usually the best method of stopping it would be to block the path of the ball in a very definite and firm way. Any half-hearted attempts to stop it won't be successful and may even help to increase its speed. Obsessions are not very different and are best tackled in a very similar way to the rolling ball.

There are several factors that can keep obsessions going ar.d make them almost impossible to stop. Here are some of the things that might be maintaining an obsession. They will need to be dealt with before doing anything else about the obsession:

- emotional distress that is not due to the obsession
- feelings of insecurity
- communication difficulties
- people 'feeding' the obsession.

The response of other people to a child's obsessions is one of the main things that keeps them going, partly by feeding into the obsessional cycle and partly by increasing the levels of tension. For example, telling a child to 'stop it' will only cause more stress. On the other hand, complying with the child's unreasonable obsessional demands is rather like giving the ball a push to make it go even faster down the hill.

The most effective method for dealing with obsessions is to 'block' them. Blocking an obsession isn't that easy, especially if it has been going for several weeks and becomes quite fixed. Obsessional thoughts are naturally more difficult to stop than compulsive behaviour. But in spite of the tendency for obsessions to continue, they do also change as time goes on and one obsession may fade away only to be replaced by another. However, if the right approach is taken and the obsessions aren't being 'fed', they can be expected gradually to become less of a problem.

'Blocking' an obsession is the most effective method for putting the brakes on. The general principle is to find a way of literally stopping the obsessional thought or the compulsive behaviour. It requires some creative ideas to find something that fits the situation. Each obsession will need to have its own individual blocking method worked out to fit it exactly and to make sense to the child. Here are some possible ways of blocking:

Checking: A child who insists on repeatedly checking might be restricted to two checks only. This will have to be carefully supervised to make sure that the child is actually putting it into practice. This approach will require the child's full co-operation. Most children complain for a while but are really pleased that someone understands what is going on and is prepared to help.

Questioning: Unfortunately, the more you give unnecessary answers, the more fixed the habit will become. It can be very difficult to resist a child's demands for an answer. There are times when parents have to go against their natural instinct to respond to their child's demands, and this is one of them.

Here are some ways of dealing with repeated questions without becoming angry or giving in:

diversions and distractions may work
saying 'I have already told you the answer'
going to another room
singing or turning on some music
turning away from your child immediately
giving a humorous answer
only answering the question once.

Cleaning: The most helpful way of blocking this compulsive behaviour is to try and disrupt it in some way. For example, allowing the child only a reasonable time to wash, such as one minute for washing hands, and limiting the time in the bathroom to 10 minutes. A clock or timer may help here. A tidying compulsion may be helped by moving things about and not allowing the house to become too tidy.

Worrying: Thoughts are particularly difficult to block, but it can be done with practice. Each child has to find the best way of doing this – it is a very individual thing. It can be done by actively stopping the worrying thought or by putting another thought in its place by 'thought control'. Some children find that by doing something else completely different it can take their mind off the thought. It is a question of experimenting and finding what works for the child and gets rid of the 'bad' thoughts.

Counting: Controlling counting is almost as difficult as blocking thoughts, but it can be done. As with all other obsessions, it will require creative ingenuity to come up with something that is reasonable, makes sense and motivates the child. Not easy, but it can be done.

Parents sometimes find it difficult to decide when to deal with an obsession and how far to go in helping the child to block it. There are three guidelines:

1. Deal with the obsession if it is interfering with your child's life.
2. Work out what would be reasonable to expect from a child of the same age without obsessions and use that as your guide.
3. Seek specialist help if the problem continues to interfere with your child's life for six weeks or more.

CONCLUSION

Mild obsessions and compulsions are not uncommon during child development. They can easily get out of control, so it is helpful to understand what they are about and to deal with them before they become too strong and fixed. Fortunately, most obsessions can be expected to resolve on their own, but if they persist and interfere with everyday life, it is advisable to obtain specialist help and advice.

6

· · · · ·

Rituals Can Be Good For You

HELPFUL RITUALS

Rituals are so much part of everyday life that we often don't realize that we are performing them. A ritual is repeated like a habit, but there are also differences. For example, most rituals are:

- more complicated
- last longer
- usually useful
- relaxing and enjoyable
- confidence-boosting.

A good example of a ritual is the regular sequence of behaviours that most people perform when they go to bed. The run up to bedtime usually follows a particular pattern with one thing following the next in a predictable way (see Chapter 3). A bedtime ritual is a good way of helping relaxation before sleeping.

The special advantage of rituals is that they reduce anxiety and uncertainty. They generate feelings of reassurance by giving an impression that the child's world is familiar and understandable. Any worries about the unknown fade into the background because the ritual takes over and becomes the main preoccupation.

Rituals are not used as much now as they were in the past, perhaps because they seem old-fashioned and unnecessary or because there isn't enough time – life is just too busy. It is likely that many of us have gone too far in rejecting rituals. There are many examples of how they can be used in a helpful way to ease us over difficult times and unfamiliar situations. Rituals are useful and can be particularly helpful at times of change, for example:

- the seasons
- night-time
- mealtimes
- deaths and births
- leaving home
- illness.

These times of change are often stressful because change involves leaving familiar things behind and facing the unknown. Rituals make the change easier to cope with because they are so predictable, well known and reassuring.

IS THERE ANY POINT TO RITUALS?

Even if you think that routines and rituals are a lot of nonsense, they can be extremely helpful for growing children who have to cope with so much change. If you think back to your own childhood you will probably find that some of the memories that give you the most pleasure are those that involved rituals.

Family rituals at bedtime and the ritual celebration of festivals are usually the events that leave the warmest memories. Holidays spent in the same place each year often develop their own rituals, where on each occasion the same things have to be repeated otherwise the holiday is not quite right.

These family rituals provide a reassuring feeling that all is well with the world and that whatever problems there are really can't be that bad. This false reassurance of rituals has given them a bad name. There is now some evidence that rituals do have an important part to play in protecting people from damaging stress, making them more able to cope with the difficulties of life. Rituals are particularly helpful for children in that they help to provide a sense of security that children need in order to feel self-confident.

ORGANIZING FAMILY RITUALS

Each parent will have experienced rituals from his or her own family background. You will be able to select the ones you would like to continue and which new ones you would like to start. It is important to plan your family rituals carefully, because they will be repeated over and over again in order to become part of your family life. And once a ritual is fixed, most children will want it to continue and won't give their parents a chance to stop it.

Here are some examples of simple rituals that parents often use at home:

Mealtimes:
- Calling the family to the table in a particular way
- Sitting in the same place at the table
- Serving people in the same order
- Saying grace

Bedtime:
- Undressing and washing in a particular sequence
- Going to bed in the same way, at the same time of day
- Saying good-night in exactly the same way every time
- Saying prayers

Weekends:
- A different routine from weekdays
- Eating special meals
- Going to bed later
- Getting up later

Birthdays:
- Having the same special food or treats
- Singing 'Happy Birthday'
- Being given 'the bumps'
- Having candles and cards

Of course there is nothing very unusual about any of these little rituals and you may not have realized that they had anything to do with rituals, but that is what they are. Children enjoy them and are helped to feel secure when carrying them out. So you may find it useful to invent your own family rituals to make life go more smoothly and to help everyone in your family feel more relaxed, secure and part of the family group.

It isn't difficult to start a new ritual. All you have to do is think of a ritual that you would like for the family – and then repeat it over and over again until other members of the family start to do it without having to be reminded. It is just a question of persevering until the ritual has become a fixed part of family life.

UNHELPFUL RITUALS

In spite of all the useful things about rituals, they can also get in the way of everyday life and become quite a nuisance. Some children and a few adults create rituals for themselves that no doubt give them a sense of security but annoy everyone else. Here are some examples of unhelpful rituals:

- always wanting to travel by the same route
- combing or fiddling with the hair over and over again
- looking in the mirror very frequently
- using the same phrase before doing something
- demanding to wear the same clothes
- making the same movements again and again
- touching surfaces or a part of the body repeatedly
- insisting on doing something unimportant in exactly the same way each time.

Although some of these rituals are rather like habits, they are more complicated and involve a larger number of different actions that build up into a pattern of behaviour. The unhelpful thing about them is that these rituals take time to perform and may seem very odd to outsiders.

These unhelpful rituals may well make the person who performs them feel good, but these feelings are very personal and not usually shared by the rest of the family. The following types of children are more likely to get stuck with unhelpful rituals:

- children with anxious and sensitive personalities
- children who are highly strung
- children who are insecure and unsettled by change
- children with poor language and/or communication skills
- children who are lonely and isolated
- children who are deaf or blind
- children with delayed development.

The repetition of familiar rituals is helpful for these children who have reason to feel more unsettled and anxious than normal. But the rituals are often performed at the cost of other people's time or wishes and they easily take over so much that the child is unable to get on with life.

DEALING WITH UNHELPFUL RITUALS

If your child has a ritual that you feel is getting in the way of your family life or interfering with the child's life, then it is worth doing something about it. Although your child may feel better for the ritual, if everyone else is upset by it then your child will also lose out and be worse off in the end.

Because rituals can interfere with development and with relationships it is reasonable to be active in stopping them. But before taking any action you should ask yourself – is the ritual:

- embarrassing?
- upsetting for the child?
- distressing to watch?
- taking up too much time?
- distracting for others?
- interfering with everyday life?

Once you have decided to stop the ritual you will have to be very firm and determined about it. Half measures don't usually work. Because stopping a ritual is hard work that has to be persisted with, you may decide that it isn't worth it. In which case the ritual will continue.

The best way of stopping rituals is to do something that makes it difficult for the child to carry them out. The plan is to disrupt the pattern of the ritual. Here are some ideas:

- Travel by different routes.
- Keep the child's hands occupied.
- Lock away mirrors or other objects involved in the ritual.
- Keep your child talking about something else.
- Keep all clothes under your control.
- Encourage other movements.

- Keep things out of reach or cover them over/up.
- Always do things slightly differently.

Don't be surprised if you manage to stop one ritual only to find it replaced by another. All this means is that your child still has a need for rituals for one of the reasons mentioned earlier. It won't always be possible to deal with the underlying cause, in which case you may be able to change the ritual in a positive way, to something that is helpful for all concerned. All that needs to be done is to make sure that the child is repeating the helpful ritual more frequently than the one that you want to stop and that the adults at home agree what the ritual should be.

CONCLUSION

Rituals are a complicated form of habit. They can be very helpful in reassuring people and making them feel secure and relaxed. However, rituals can also get in the way and become a handicap. Rituals can be stopped and new ones made without too much difficulty – once you know how!

7
· · · · ·

Questions and Answers

Parents usually ask two types of questions when they have been given some advice. 'Yes, but...' is what you are likely to say if you are not really convinced that the advice is correct and you can think of all kinds of reasons why you should not believe it, or if you think that I have missed something. The other type of question is: 'What if...?' – asked by parents who think the advice seems sensible but who can see all the reasons why it might not work.

YES, BUT...

'I hardly agree with anything you have said'

Well, everybody is entitled to his or her own views! There are a wide range of ideas about childcare and many different ways of bringing children up. There is no 'best way' because each individual has different needs. What works with one family may not work with another. I have tried to outline what the main issues are and what the underlying mechanisms are, so that you can work things out for yourself. If your child is still young, it is possible to make lots of mistakes without too many irreversible effects. But later on, as children approach adolescence, any earlier mistakes in child-rearing tend to become more obvious.

The ideas and guidelines in this book are based on a lot of people's experience and the results of research. What I can say is that the approach described here is more likely to work with most children than any other method.

'You have said nothing much about bedwetting, surely this is an important habit that many children have'

Bedwetting certainly is a common habit that affects 10 per cent of five year olds and 5 per cent of 10 year olds. However, it is mainly due to developmental immaturity and I have therefore dealt with it in my book *Growth and Development* in this series.

'My daughter has sores on her legs that the doctor thinks she has caused through a scratching habit. I don't believe it'

Once a child has a sore place for whatever reason, it isn't unusual for a habit of fiddling with the sore to develop. The fiddling is often obvious and not difficult to stop, but occasionally the child is never seen touching the sores but they continue in spite of everything. There are several possible causes, but one that should be considered is *dermatitis artifacta* (see next question). If there is any doubt about what is delaying healing you should get help from a specialist.

'What is dermatitis artifacta?'

Some children get into a habit of scratching their skin so frequently or so hard that it makes it sore, even to the point of bleeding. The habit may develop into a ritual or obsession and leave such unsightly marks that it is difficult to imagine that any child could possibly do something like that. It is unusual actually to see a child scratch and it may occur during the night, during the half-asleep–half-awake stage.

Dermatitis artifacta is rare, but is more often seen in girls than in boys. It tends to occur when there is some cause for tension and distress and requires specialist knowledge to diagnose. Removal of any obvious stress factors may help, but once started the irritation of the condition itself will sometimes keep the scratching habit going. In this case you can try filing the nails daily so that they do less damage and find some way of covering the affected parts with clothes, plasters or bandages so that they are protected.

'You haven't mentioned masturbation. Surely this can become a nasty habit'

As young boys and girls learn to explore their bodies, they soon find their private parts or 'genitals'. Some but not all children find that if they touch or rub these parts repeatedly, interesting and pleasant sensations are produced. Once they have discovered this and had an opportunity to repeat it several times it can easily become a habit.

Of course, children have no understanding of the strong emotions that public masturbation can cause so they often find the reactions of adults around them even more interesting than what they are doing themselves. They may repeat the masturbation just to get a reaction from others who see them do it.

It may help to think of masturbation as being rather like picking the nose – it may feel good, but is not something that most parents want to encourage. And although there is no harm in masturbation or nose-picking, it is best for both to be done in private.

Masturbation is more likely to occur in children who are bored or unstimulated, so it will obviously help if they can be kept busy and interested in other things. Young children under three years old are best dealt with by making access to the genitals difficult. This can be done by using an all-in-one suit that does up at the back and by putting the child in several layers of clothes.

Older children will require a simple and clear statement that this sort of behaviour is not acceptable in public. It is important to keep emotions out of this. If your child picks up any emotions the result will either be a sense of guilt and confusion or additional pleasure in producing emotional reactions in others.

By five to seven years of age most children have a strong sense of privacy and masturbation in public is likely to have a deeper significance that needs to be investigated further. At this stage it would be advisable to consult a children's specialist.

---

*'I disagree that washing and dressing have anything
to do with habits'*

There are many daily tasks that are repeated so frequently that we do them without thinking but always in the same way, which are the same characteristics as for a habit. Although we tend to think of habits as useless, I think it is helpful to see repeated useful behaviours as habits also.

It is helpful to look at many childhood behaviours that occur frequently as habits. Even things like tempers or stealing can be understood in this way. It reminds us that some behaviours happen automatically because they have been repeated so frequently in the past. It is also a reminder that any behaviour that has become a habit is going to be difficult to stop – just as difficult as it is to stop nail-biting or smoking.

---

*'I haven't been able to teach my four-year-old son to have
the good habit of sitting still, even for a few minutes'*

The habit of being still is best started from an early stage when
children are still small enough to be held in their parents'
arms. Although some children are much more restless than
others, they can all be helped by being held calmly for a few
minutes.

It isn't too late to teach a restless four year old to be still.
There are several different ways of doing this, but the general
principle is the same: the control must come from outside
before self-control can develop. There is an effective cuddle-
hold method that some parents discover for themselves. It is
not right for every child or every parent but it can be extremely helpful in some cases.

The cuddle-hold method of helping restless children develop
the habit of being still works like this:

- Only use it on children about whom you feel
  confident that you can comfortably control physically.
- You have to decide for how long you are going to
  cuddle-hold your child. Five to 10 minutes would be
  a reasonable time.
- Don't let your child make the decisions about this.
  This is one time when you have to be in total
  control.
- Sit the child on your lap, facing away from you so
  that your face cannot be seen and so that there are
  no other distractions.
- Put your arms around the child's trunk/tummy and
  with your left hand hold the child's right wrist. Then
  with your right hand hold the child's left wrist.
- Now cross your child's arms over so that your arms
  are uncrossed. To do this you will have to pull

firmly but only hard enough to keep your arms in a position on either side of the child's hips.

- Your child's legs should be between your legs, which should be crossed at the ankles so that you can grip your child's legs firmly enough to prevent them thrashing around.
- When your child wriggles and struggles, you should tighten your grip just enough to control the child and prevent an escape. When your child is still, you can relax your hold. But don't leave go and be prepared to tighten your grip if there is another wriggle.
- When the time has come to end the cuddle-hold it is best to end at a time when your child is still and then leave go, saying 'That is good, well done' or something similar.

Most restless children don't like the cuddle-hold at first. They will usually cry, scream, fight and bite until they realize that they can't just do what they like all the time. After a cuddle-holding session you will almost always find that your child is able to stay calm and still for a longer time than before.

The cuddle-hold training for a habit of being still needs to be repeated as many times as it takes for the new habit of being still to become established. Once or twice a day or even less often will produce results quite quickly in most children.

'I have done everything you say, but it doesn't work!'

Well done! The guidelines that I have given are tried and tested and can be expected to be successful if applied in a consistent and determined way. If you have done all this for several months without any improvement then something is wrong somewhere. Maybe all your hard work is being undermined by another person or perhaps your child is very difficult. Think about what I have written and discuss it with a friend, read the book again and if you are still stuck, this is the time to get some professional help.

'My five-year-old daughter has been waking screaming and terrified an hour or two after going to sleep. Could this be a sleep habit?'

It sounds as though your daughter may have night terrors, which are not usually considered to be a sleep habit. But they do occur at a time when daytime habits are common and like habits, they can become more frequent if too much attention is paid to them.

Children with night terrors wake up suddenly, with eyes that are often open and staring. Screaming out and pointing, with a frightened expression on their face, is not unusual. Any words spoken are brief and indicate terrifying experiences related to aggression or the threat of death such as 'the monster will get me.'

About 5 per cent of children have night terrors, with a peak age of four to seven years of age, but probably no age is exempt. Night terrors are more common during the first third of the night and the same children are more likely to go on to sleep-walking at some stage.

Night terrors occur during the deeper stages of sleep and are therefore not remembered by the child on waking the next day. This differentiates night terrors from nightmares which are, of course, all too well remembered.

The best way of responding to night terrors is to return the child to sleep with the minimum of disturbance. It is important not to attempt to wake your daughter up, but rather to use the minimum of intervention to tuck her up in bed again. This is one of the times when it is helpful to have a familiar night-time phrase that is used regularly when saying good-night. The more attempts to wake the child up or actively to pacify her, the more likely it is that the problem will continue. In cases where the night terrors are causing concern due to their frequency it often helps to keep a record of the times when the episodes occur and if the problem continues, briefly wake your daughter shortly before the night terror is most likely to occur. This seems to disrupt sleep habit patterns and after two or three nights of waking the terrors have usually faded away.

'My 12-year-old son has the habit of sleep-walking'

Sleep-walking occurs at the same stages of deep sleep as night terrors. It occurs in about 15 per cent of children and about a third of these have a regular habit of walking in their sleep. It has been reported in very young toddlers but reaches a peak between 10 and 14 years of age. Children who walk in their sleep are more likely to have previously had one or more of the following sleep problems:

- restless sleep
- bedwetting
- night terrors
- sleep-talking
- a family history of sleep-walking.

Sleep-walking can be dealt with in much the same way as night terrors. However, it is also important to make sure that the bedroom, the windows and doors in the house are secure and safe. It may help to use some form of burglar alarm so that you know when your son is out of bed if you usually sleep through his wanderings.

Because children who sleep-walk are usually deeply asleep it is best not to try and wake them, but to simply steer them gently back to bed with reassuring words and tuck them up with your usual good-night phrase.

Contrary to popular belief, sleep-walking and night terrors have no particular significance. There is no evidence that sleep-walking or night terrors indicate deep psychological problems. They occur in perfectly normal children, but occur more frequently if a child is distressed or excited for any reason.

'What can I do about my son's repeated nightmares?'

Nightmares are common and probably occur in very young children as well as throughout childhood and adolescence. Some 30 per cent of children report at least one bad dream within the last month. Nightmares may happen at any stage of sleep but most of the remembered dreams occur in the latter half of the night during the lighter stages of sleep, which makes them easier to remember.

The experience can be very vivid and is not infrequently linked to a recent traumatic experience. For example, doing something wrong, seeing something upsetting on the TV or being worried about something. Occasionally the nightmare is so upsetting that a child may refuse to go to bed at all.

Nightmares and other sleep disturbances occur more frequently when a child is distressed for any reason, but all sleep disorders are so common in undisturbed children that it is unhelpful to assume that nightmares must be a sign of psychological distress.

Children often find recurrent nightmares and other dreams surprisingly easy to control if they are encouraged to believe that this is possible. For example, a repeated nightmare about a vicious dog could be brought to an end by putting a cage round the animal — a dream about drowning could be concluded by someone throwing a lifebelt and so on. The dream resolution needs to be repeatedly practised before going to sleep until it is effective. If all else fails your son could always learn to terminate a dream by waking up!

Try and avoid responding too quickly to your son's nightmares. Early and repeated parental interventions are likely to increase the frequency of nightmares and establish them as part of the normal sleep habit. If your son is clearly in distress, your response should be limited to the minimum required to quieten him. A few reassuring words together with the good-night tucking up ritual should be enough. If possible, it is best to avoid taking a child into the parental bed since this can so easily become a fixed habit.

'My four-year-old daughter has a habit of calling out after I have put her to bed'

Children are often very skilled at thinking up all sorts of reasons why they might need to call out, even though they and their parents know that there is no need for it. I expect your daughter has tried all of the following:

- I want a drink.
- I am too hot/cold.
- My head/tummy/legs ache.
- I have seen a monster.
- What are you doing?
- Can I go to the toilet?
- Mummy!...Daddy!
- Good-night!...Say good-night to me!

Of course it is very difficult not to reply, but if you are sure that your daughter has no need to call out and is just trying to keep your attention, then you should not reply. This is yet another time when it is best to go against your natural instinct, which would be to respond to your daughter. But if you do respond you will soon find that your daughter has got you into a habit of always fitting in with her night-time demands and her habit will grow stronger and stronger.

Just being quiet when your daughter calls out won't be easy, but if you have decided it is the right thing to do, and you stick at it, you will soon find that her calling out habit fades away quickly in a few days. And no harm will have come to your daughter. In fact you will probably find that she is more reasonable and less demanding during the daytime as well.

WHAT IF...?

'My son has developed a habit of coughing even though he seems to be quite well'

Many children go through a phase of coughing repeatedly. This usually starts with a genuine cough that goes on after the illness has passed.

Sometimes the cough is obviously attention-seeking, but usually there is no apparent reason for the cough. Nevertheless there are other less obvious causes that you should consider:

- Mild asthma can cause a short unproductive cough.
- Whooping cough may leave a persistent cough.
- Large tonsils may tickle the back of the throat and cause coughing.
- 'Catarrh' or mucus in the nose and sinuses can drip down the back of the throat and cause coughing that is worse on lying down.
- Repeated coughing may take the form of a tic, either alone or with other tics.

All these causes of repeated coughing are beyond the control of the child, so telling your son to stop coughing is to expect too much. There may be something that you can do to improve the underlying cause and if in any doubt you should get medical advice. Unfortunately, cough mixtures are of little more that psychological benefit although simple remedies like steam inhalations may help. Generally it is best to take as little notice of the cough as you can – then at least it won't be used to get attention.

'My daughter has a habit of sneezing repeatedly'

Repeated sneezing is common in children with hay fever. Sometimes the allergy can be very mild but the sneezing both dramatic and frequent. Although there may be various physical causes for this that need to be checked out by your doctor, sneezing is also a good way of getting attention. If you think that your daughter is making a drama of the sneezing, then it is best ignored or she can be taught how to stop a sneeze by pressing on the soft part of the nose.

'My son has hiccups so frequently, it seems like a habit'

Hiccups have more to do with an irritation of the nerves to the diaphragm than with habits. Hiccups do occasionally become stuck as a habit, especially if they provoke a big reaction from other people.

I have discovered a way of stopping hiccups that is much easier than drinking out of the wrong side of a cup, drinking upside down or any of the other patent remedies, but it only works if you can catch it after the first or second hiccup. Here is what anyone can try as soon as the first hiccup comes:

- Stop whatever you are doing.
- Stand up straight.
- Take a deep breath in,
- And then breathe right out – slowly.
- Relax as much as you can as you breathe out.
- Hold your breath after breathing out.

If all has gone well you should feel a little sensation of trapped air coming up the gullet from the stomach. If you feel this it is most unlikely that you will hiccup again on that occasion. If you feel nothing, it is worth repeating the procedure again, but after three hiccups it probably won't work and you may have to stand on your head drinking from the wrong side of a cup – or you could just wait for it to pass!

'My 10-year-old daughter has a habit of pulling her hair out'

The habit of hair-pulling is called *tricholomania*, which sounds worse than it is. Many children have a hair-twiddling habit and it is only a few who actually pull it out as well, leaving bare patches. There are other causes of these bare patches so you should get your daughter seen by your doctor. Sometimes the patches are a mystery, but if you have seen her pulling or fiddling with her hair it is quite likely that she has tricholomania. If this is the case then any of the usual methods of habit-stopping may work (see Chapter 2).

One of the most effective ways of stopping hair-fiddling is to cut the hair short so that it is difficult to pull at. It should be possible to do this and still keep the hair attractive and fashionable. Failing this, a hat or head scarf may help to stop the habit.

'I have done everything you have suggested, but my child still has serious problems. I think I need professional help for him'

It is always difficult to know when is the right time to get professional help with a child and/or family problem, and even more difficult to know where to go and whom to ask. Here are some suggestions if you feel it is necessary to get some outside help:

- Ask other parents and professionals what they know of the local services, but take what they say with a pinch of salt, because individual opinions may be unreliable. One of the best informed people is likely to be your GP.
- Voluntary groups for parents can be very supportive and give you an idea of how other people have coped. But they don't give professional advice, although they should be able to advise on how to get this type of help.
- There is a wide range of professional groups who have specialized training and experience with family relationship problems. The difference between the various professions is confusing to say the least. One way round this problem is to ask your GP to refer the family to the local Child Psychiatry Service, where it is usual for a range of different professionals to work closely together.
- Don't be put off by a referral to a consultant child psychiatrist. They are medically qualified doctors with a very broad training in the full range of child and family problems. They have special skills in helping any problem of emotions, behaviour or relationships that seems to be getting out of control and out of proportion to what might be expected in the circumstances.

100

What the Research Shows

Most of the research on habits has focused on tics and obsessions rather than ordinary, everyday habits and routines. However, there have been some very interesting developments in the research on obsessions and tics recently and it seems likely that ordinary habits are at the mild end of the same continuum. So the research on obsessions may well give some understanding about the nature of 'normal' habits.

SURVEYS

National Surveys of all children born in Britain in one week in 1958 and 1970 have found the following rates of habits when the children were followed up at five years old:

- Nail-biting: 30 per cent
- Thumb-sucking: 30 per cent
- Eating problems: 36 per cent
- Sleep problems: 25 per cent
- Tics and twitches: 4 per cent.

At seven years of age the rate of twitches and tics had doubled, nail-biting was just as frequent and thumb-sucking was less frequent. Both nail-biting and thumb-sucking were more likely to occur in girls than boys. Children who bit their nails had an increased risk of having an accident and to have unclear speech, but the reasons for these associations are complex (Golding and Rush, 1986).

In the same survey Golding (1986) found that children with sleeping and feeding problems were more likely to have:

- no siblings (i.e. to be the first-born child)
- sleeping problems as infants
- health problems
- moved house
- toilet training problems
- temper tantrums.

An investigation of all children aged nine, 10 and 11 years old living on the Isle of Wight (Rutter et al., 1970) showed that thumb-sucking decreases as children grow older and the frequency of nail-biting increases. In the same study, twitches and stuttering were found to be more common in boys than girls. An important American study of childhood symptoms found that about 10 per cent had tics at some stage of their development (MacFarlane et al., 1954). A review of the research on tics by Corbett and Turpin (1985) noted that some studies reported that up to one in four children may experience tics at some time and that boys were at least twice as likely to have tics than girls.

THUMB-SUCKING

Although thumb- and finger-sucking under the age of three years is generally considered quite normal, there is strong evidence that after four years it causes orthodontic problems that increase as the sucking continues. Christensen and Sanders (1987) in Australia have investigated this problem and from a review of the research on thumb-sucking concluded that it might cause:

- malformation of the mouth and face
- difficulty in responding to questions
- interference with spontaneous speech
- restricted use of play material
- negative interactions with parents.

Some studies suggest that frequent feeding in early infancy and late weaning, together with lack of stimulation when an infant is put to bed, may be associated with an increased rate of thumb-sucking (Dunn, 1980). The evidence for the causes and results of problem thumb-sucking requires further research.

Christensen and Sanders (1987) have reported an effective method for stopping thumb-sucking that involves a co-operative effort between parent and child. The times and the circumstances when the child is most likely to thumb-suck are first identified. Then the child is taught to make a clenched fist with the thumb inside the fist and to hold it there for a count of 20. The child is expected to do this at the first sign of anything that might lead to thumb-sucking and if the child is found sucking at any time then the fist-clenching has to be repeated once. Ten days are devoted to this training procedure and should it be unsuccessful it can be repeated at a later date. The same approach could be used for nail-biting.

TICS

The review by Corbett and Turpin (1985) reported that the usual onset of childhood tics is between two and 15 years, with a peak at around seven years old.

The same review reported that tics were linked with the following conditions:

- overactive behaviour
- a family history of tics (about 15 per cent)

- other habits
- speech disorders
- obsessions
- emotional problems.

A review from America (Cohen et al., 1985) suggests that there is evidence that stimulants may cause tics in children with a family history of tics. Almost all the neurotransmitter chemical systems in the brain have been implicated in the production of tics and it seems likely that a complex interaction occurs between physiological, psychological, genetic and environmental factors that eventually leads to the formation of tics.

Corbett and Turpin (1985) also reviewed the research on a severe form of tics called Gilles de la Tourette Syndrome. This involves multiple and complex twitches that are often associated with sounds, swear words or phrases uttered by the child. Fortunately the condition is rare (probably less than 1 in 1000). Follow-up studies of simple tics and Tourette Syndrome shows that they tend to improve with time and as few as 6 per cent of the severe cases continue into adult life. However, the condition can be debilitating and many secondary emotional and social effects can be caused by the tic. Because spontaneous improvement is usual, no specific treatment is necessary unless there are significant problems.

Drugs that affect the level of neurotransmitters in the brain have been shown to be the most effective treatment, but they do have side-effects that have to be balanced against the adverse effects of the symptoms. Another form of treatment that has been recommended involves the child repeating the movement of the tic over and over again until the muscles become too tired to tic. Unfortunately this approach has not been found to be effective in most cases.

Various other treatments include relaxation, recording and monitoring, but support and reassurance from somebody who is well informed about tics is probably the most helpful of all.

OBSESSIONS

The true prevalence of obsessions is not known because many children prefer to keep them secret. Obsessions that are so severe that they interfere with everyday life. They occur in less than 1 per cent of children (Rapoport, 1986). Judith Rapoport has reviewed the research on obsessions and investigated a group of obsessional children at the National Institute of Mental Health in the US. She identified an interesting group of 'super normals' who were obsessional but they were not particularly disturbed by their symptoms and were ambitious, energetic high achievers. In contrast to this was the finding that many young people with an obsessional disorder had other associated symptoms including:

- depression and anxiety symptoms
- tics and twitches
- anorexia nervosa
- a family history of obsessions
- mild neurological problems
- disruptive behaviour
- a rigid, striving personality.

Another reviewer of the research (Hersov, 1985) reported that the obsessional symptoms usually start around six years of age and that there is a close association with phobias in more than half the cases. Indeed, obsessions can also be seen as phobias; for example a washing obsession could also be called a dirt phobia.

Treatment involves dealing with any obvious stress factors and focusing on preventing or blocking the obsession using behavioural methods. Recently, there have been promising developments in the drug treatment of the more severe and disabling obsessions (Rapoport, 1986). Generally the outcome of mild obsessional behaviour in childhood is good, but a follow-up of children with severe obsessions (Zeitlin, 1986) has shown that there is a strong tendency for the symptoms to occur in a similar form in adult life.

STEREOTYPIES

'Stereotypies' is the technical term for repetitive rhythmic movements that are purposeful and apparently under voluntary control. Like habits, rituals and obsessions they are able to relieve tension. The following repetitive behaviour would be considered to be stereotyped behaviour:

- head-banging and head-shaking
- rocking and swaying
- sucking and teeth-grinding
- stroking and touching
- twisting and twirling
- scratching and pinching.

A research review by Werry et al. (1983) indicates that about one in five preschool children has stereotypies. As children grow older they tend to grow out of these rhythmic movements and may then become involved in influencing their environment in other ways, by moving objects or by controlling people. Five main factors were identified to explain the cause of stereotypies:

1. Under-stimulation and sensory deprivation (blindness and deafness)
2. Over-stimulation, excitement or distress
3. Neuromuscular dysfunction
4. Learned behaviour due to rewards resulting from the stereotypies
5. Normal developmental processes

The authors conclude that rhythmic, stereotyped behaviour probably has a useful function in preparing muscles and co-ordination during development, but the behaviour may persist for longer than normal under certain abnormal conditions. Treatment needs to be aimed at the underlying causes outlined above.

SLEEPING AND EATING HABITS

Many of the behaviours associated with eating and sleeping can be trained into good habit routines quite early on in a child's life. Difficulties may arise if these habits are not reasonably well established within the first two to three years and there is evidence that early feeding and sleeping problems are likely to continue in about 50 per cent of children (Golding, 1986). In this case mealtimes and bedtimes are likely to be demanding events for parents. The way in which children adapt to family routines is partly dependent on their temperament. Those with strongly negative moods who are slow to adapt to change have been shown to have more difficulty getting into good sleeping and eating habits (Thomas and Chess, 1977).

An excellent review of the research on the development of feeding and sleeping patterns in childhood by Dunn (1980) suggests that early experience is important. Babies who are put to the breast early on are said to be easier to feed in later months. A rigid four-hourly feeding routine early on does not seem to suit many young babies, especially those who are breastfed, who often need to be fed more frequently. Later on, feeding routines become more important in preparing the way for later eating problems. For example, over-feeding in the first six months has been found to be linked with adult obesity (Crisp et al., 1970).

A regular sleep pattern is affected by what is happening in the environment and childcare routines. By two and a half years old most children have established a sleep routine, but those that haven't are more likely to have had a difficult birth and to have experienced other adversities (Dunn, 1980).

Richman et al. (1985) compared drugs as treatment for sleep problems and found that they were less effective than a behavioural method that involves negotiating an agreement with parents to leave their children to sleep alone at night and not go into them. (The approach is rather similar to that outlined in Chapter 3). Children with night-waking problems are likely to continue with the same ones for several years (Bax, 1980). In older children there is some evidence that sleep problems are linked with later problems in adult life (Zeitlin, 1986).

References
. . . . .

M. C. O. Bax, 'Sleep disturbance in the young child', *British Medical Journal* 2, pp. 1177–79.

A. P. Christensen and M. R. Sanders, 'Habit reversal and differential reinforcement of other behaviour in the treatment of thumb-sucking: an analysis of generalization and side effects', *Journal of Child Psychol. Psychiatry* 28 (1987), pp. 281–96.

D. J. Cohen, J. F. Leckman and B. A. Shaywitz, 'The Tourette Syndrome and other tics', in D. Shaffer, A. Ehrhardt and L. Greenhill (eds), *The Clinical Guide to Child Psychiatry* (London: The Free Press, 1985).

J. A. Corbett and G. Turpin, 'Tics and Tourette's Syndrome', in M. Rutter and L. Hersov (eds), *Child and Adolescent Psychiatry: Modern Approaches* (London: Blackwell Scientific, 1985).

A. H. Crisp, J. W. B. Douglas, J. M. Ross and E. Stonehill, 'Some developmental aspects of disorders of weight', *Journal of Psychosomatic Medicine* 14 (1970), pp. 327–45.

J. F. Dunn, 'Feeding and Sleeping', in M. Rutter (ed.), *Scientific Foundations of Developmental Psychiatry* (London: Heinemann, 1980).

J. Golding, 'Feeding and Sleeping Problems', in N. R. Butler and J. Golding (eds), *From Birth to Five* (Oxford: Pergamon Press, 1986).

J. Golding and D. Rush, 'Temper tantrums and other behaviour problems', in N. R. Butler and J. Golding (eds), *From Birth to Five* (Oxford: Pergamon Press, 1986).

L. Hersov, 'Emotional Disorders', in M. Rutter and L. Hersov (eds), *Child and Adolescent Psychiatry: Modern Approaches* (London: Blackwell Scientific, 1985).

J. W. MacFarlane, L. Allen and M. P. Honzik, *A Developmental Study of the Behaviour Problems of Normal Children Between 21 Months and 14 Years* (Berkeley, CA: University of California Press, 1954).

J. L. Rapoport, 'Childhood obsessive compulsive disorders', *Journal of Child Psychol. Psychiatry* 27 (1986), pp. 289–95.

N. Richman, J. Douglas, H. Hunt, R. Lansdown and R. Levere, 'Behavioural methods in the treatment of sleep disorders – a pilot study', *Journal of Child Psychol. Psychiatry* 26 (1985), pp. 581–90.

M. Rutter, J. Tizard and K. Whitmore (eds), *Education, Health and Behaviour* (London: Longmans, 1970; reprint New York: Robert Krieger Publishing, 1981).

A. Thomas and S. Chess, *Temperament and Development* (New York: Brunner/Mazel, 1977).

J. S. Werry, 'Physical illness and allied disorders', in H. Quay and J. S. Werry (eds), *Psychopathological Disorders of Childhood* (New York, Wiley, 1986).

H. Zeitlin, *The Natural History of Psychiatric Disorder in Children* (Oxford: Maudsley Monograph, Oxford University Press, 1986).

FURTHER READING

C. Guilleminault (ed.), *Sleep and Its Disorders in Children* (New York: Raven Press, 1987).
A detailed and technical book, but nothing on treatment.

M. Rutter (ed.), *Scientific Foundations of Developmental Psychiatry* (London: Heinemann, 1980).
An excellent reference book on the wider aspects of child development.

Index

· · · · ·